The Assessment HANDBOOK

Lynn Cousins • Jacquie Buttriss

Ann Callander • Colin Rouse

pfp publishing limited

© pfp publishing limited 2004

First published in Britain in 2004 by
pfp publishing limited
67–71 Goswell Road
London EC1V 7EP

Writers Lynn Cousins, Jacquie Buttriss, Ann Callander, Colin Rouse

Design PinkFrog

Project management *specialist* publishing services ltd, Milton Keynes

Photography Nicholas James and Educational Solutions

Printed and bound in the UK.

A catalogue record for this book is available from the British Library.

All rights reserved. No part of this publication may be reproduced, stored in a retrieval system, copied or transmitted without written permission from the publisher except that the materials may be photocopied for use within the purchasing institution only.

ISBN 1 904677 02 9

pfp orders and customer services
FREEPOST 59
Rochester ME2 4BR

Tel: 0870 241 0731 Fax: 0870 241 2765
www.pfp-publishing.com

CONTENTS

About this book — 4

Introduction — 5

1 Focus on assessment — 10

2 Learning styles — 16

3 Tracking progress — 24

4 Assessment for special purposes — 31

5 Using summative assessment — 40

6 Marking for ongoing assessment — 46

7 The assessment of skills — 52

8 Assessment and planning — 59

9 Involving children in their own assessment — 67

10 Involving parents in the assessment process — 72

Appendices — 76

References — 79

About this book

This handbook is about the assessment that starts on Monday morning. It is about gathering information in focused ways every day of the year. It is about knowing what you want to find out and how you intend to go about it. It is about using that information in practical ways to support your planning and teaching, and to assist the child's future learning. If national tests, or end of year assessments, are to be useful, they should be valid interpretations of a child's achievements over the year. They should build on the knowledge you have amassed about children and their learning over the whole of the year.

It is about assessment for learning and for finding out how each child learns. The more information you have about the way that children learn, and the knowledge and skills they already possess, then the more effectively you can teach them and enable greater learning to take place. Through understanding learning styles you can aim to provide something for everyone over a block of lessons, so that each child is working and learning at his or her optimum level.

It is about involving parents in the assessment of their child whenever that is appropriate. If parents have opportunities to give information as well as hear it, they can be encouraged to play their part in recognising their own child's achievements. When home and school work in cooperation, sharing their knowledge and utilising the strengths they each possess, then the child will feel a greater sense of security. As a result of this there can be rewards such as an improvement in levels of self-esteem, behaviour and the approach to learning and school in general.

It is about enabling every child in your class to succeed at the peak of their capabilities, whatever their home circumstances, social setting or any special needs they may have. It is about challenging gifted children, recognising what they have to offer and where they need help. It is about the quality of your planning and delivery so that you make sure they meet the needs of each child.

It is about tracking the rate of progress of every child in your class. When you can see the pattern of their learning you can intervene to address concerns, you can move some children on at a faster rate, you can adapt your teaching style or content.

It is about involving the children in the process, enabling them to become partners in their own assessment. Children can learn assessment skills, they can learn how to judge their own work and work with their peers to recognise achievements and identify aspects that need further development.

It is about gathering and using information in a rigorous, systematic way, so that your teaching will be continually improving. It can be a part of your own professional development, recognised in your performance management targets.

In other words, this handbook is about assessment as an integral part of every lesson of every day.

Introduction

Assessment is a whole-school issue, fundamental to the success of the teaching and learning that goes on in any school.

As far back as 1988 it was recognised that assessment lies at the heart of education.

> 'Promoting children's learning is the principal aim of schools. Assessment lies at the heart of this process. It can provide a framework in which the educational objectives can be set and pupils' progress charted and expressed. It can yield a basis for planning the next step in response to children's needs … It should be an integral part of the educational process, continually providing "feedback" and "feed forward". It therefore needs to be incorporated systematically into teaching strategies and practices at all levels.'
> (TGAT, 1988).

There is a requirement for every school to have a policy for assessment and to carry out assessment in all its different forms as one way of monitoring and evaluating the effectiveness of the school. Some schools have assessment coordinators, and they or the headteacher will instigate the writing of this policy, and make sure that it is regularly reviewed to reflect current theories, DfES requirements and the good practice in the school. Before you can contribute to the discussion you need to have read about the theory of assessment, and thought about it in terms of your own children. This book is intended as a practical guide but there is a list of additional reading on page 63.

As a quick reminder, this introduction

- sums up why you need to assess the children
- suggests what forms assessment can take
- summarises where it fits in the learning process
- provides guidance for a policy statement on assessment for your school.

Why do we assess children?

We need to know what the children already know if the learning we are to offer them is to move them on to the next stage or level.

> 'The most important single factor influencing learning is what the learner already knows.'
> (Bennett and Kell, 1989, p29)

It may be acceptable for long-term and even medium-term plans to reflect the expected levels of the year group, but short-term plans must be more accurate than this. Each year you will need to modify the plans you wrote last year to match the cohort of children in this class. You will have to take the broad picture given in the medium-term planning and make it fit the children you are now teaching in your short-term plans.

How do you know how this modification will occur, or what changes to make unless you have some prior knowledge of what the children already know? The first assessment you will undertake will be to furnish you with this knowledge. You might do this simply by reading the results of earlier assessments – as carried out by the previous teacher or the pre-school provider. You might brainstorm with the children to find out their existing understanding of a topic of work. You can draw mind-maps to show this. You can devise an activity that allows the children to demonstrate their current skill level.

Once you know where the children are, you can plan tasks and activities that will take them through the next stages. You will be able to plan appropriate work. You will be able to plot the targets for the children to achieve during this next unit of work.

However you choose to do this, involve the children. They can then become part of the assessment process and be aware of their own learning. They can take a pride in the skills and knowledge they already possess and may be able to anticipate their future learning needs.

Make sure that you add the tasks and activities you have chosen to do, to your medium-term plans, so allowing time to carry out the assessment and reflect on it before you launch into a new area of learning with the children. This should be seen as part of the work that you do and not treated as an add-on extra that has to be fitted into spare moments. Allow time for it. Make it important.

We need to know how the children learn, if we are to provide them with the optimal opportunities for learning.

> 'respect individuality and ... engage the attentional systems'
> (Smith, 2002, p145)

You can read many books or attend courses that will explain the different ways that people learn. Your school may have a chosen approach that you have to keep to. But you need to be able to identify how individual children in your class learn if you are to use these theories effectively. Is George a visual learner? Does Mary rely on kinaesthetic learning? Nisha finds it easy to access spatial intelligence but struggles with activities involving logical–mathematical intelligence. How can I use this strength to help her understand other concepts?

Plan some assessments to enable you to determine children's preferred learning styles. These will usually be by observation of children as they carry out set tasks, and by noticing those tasks that allow highest achievement for individual children. Are there any children who you know to be generally capable but who are not achieving as you would expect in certain areas of the curriculum? You can also give time during assessments to talk with the children and to encourage them to explain how the work they have done helped them, or not, to understand the concept or skill being taught.

As part of this 'how children learn', we need also to look at the processes and strategies which the children are using, not just the end product. So a lot of assessment in your classroom needs to happen through observation of children as they carry out their tasks, by analysing the process they used, by talking to them to find out the thought processes which were involved. This helps you to pinpoint the causes of any difficulty or to demonstrate other effective ways to approach a task.

There is a

> '...tendency among teachers to limit the assessments to the products of the children's work. Rarely did they attempt to ascertain the processes or strategies deployed by children in coming to their finished product.'
> (Bennett and Kell, 1989, p29)

Use this knowledge to broaden the scope of the activities you offer the children. Different children will learn in different ways. You will have your own preferred learning and teaching style. Look through your plans and adapt them so that you offer a variety, and something for everyone over the range of work.

We need to find out what the children have learned so that we can plan for their future needs and adapt our teaching if necessary.

When you assess children's learning following one individual lesson or at the end of a unit of work, you can find out

> '...how the children stand in relation to each other, which pupils need special help, how far the class has progressed, and to what extent the teacher has made himself understood.'
> (Gillett and Sadler, 1962, p52)

In fact you can find out so many things that you can struggle to make sense of it, or record or use the information in any meaningful way. So think first about what you want to know – are you checking acquisition of knowledge or of skills, or the level of understanding? Fine-tune this to the particular skills and so on. Having decided what you want to assess, find a task or a test that will enable you to find it out in a straightforward way.

> 'Ensure that you are certain of the purpose of the test and aware of the specific skills it examines.'
> (Moyle, 1972, p189)

If assessment is to be useful it must be specific and focused. Think about what you want to find out and how you will do it. Be precise and you will end up with a focused assessment and a useful gauge of learning. Include the assessment activities in your plans and allow time for completing them.

Use the information to measure individual, group or class targets and set new ones. Or make a note on your planning to remind yourself of a gap that needs to be attended to next time you cover this work, or a change that needs to be made to the planning of the activities in content or presentation.

We need to know why certain children are struggling to achieve. There will be times when you want to assess children in order to diagnose their learning or their skills development, in order to find out why they are struggling and how you can help them to achieve. Diagnostic assessment is a specialised field and relies on published tests which have to be used accurately and with training in many instances. Use these with care, taking advice from your SEN coordinator and other advisory staff.

What forms can assessment take?

Assessment breaks down into the four main types

- summative
- formative
- diagnostic
- evaluative.

Summative assessments give information at the end of a defined period of time, and provide snapshots of how the child is doing at any particular time.

They are carried out periodically and will show you how children have progressed, what they have achieved and provide the information you need to work out what their next steps will be. They are usually written for the benefit of someone else – the next teacher or the parents.

You can use them to see how a whole group of children are working and judge progress against fixed criteria. They include end of year tests, national tests, and the Foundation Stage Profile.

Formative assessments feed forwards into the provision of the next suitable learning experiences.

These are going on every day. When children start an activity you explain to them what they should be able to do or know by the time they have completed the activity, ie. the learning objective.

When children have completed the activity you give feedback to let them know how well they have done, reminding them of the objective and explaining what they now can do or know. With older children this may include written comments in their books. Although these can have a limited impact with young children, they can be a useful reminder to you or to a parent looking back through their child's work. However, it should always be accompanied by verbal, one-to-one feedback.

This is also a time when you can look at personal targets and how they have been reached or what the child needs to do next if they are to reach the targets agreed for them.

You should also tell them what they will be doing next time, so that they get to know, or are able to do, something else. If the child hasn't been successful with the task and hasn't achieved the objective, you can explain that next time they will be trying it another way so that they have another chance to show what they can do or learn. In this way the child becomes aware of the process of self-assessment, and is set on the road to becoming an independent learner.

Diagnostic assessments give information that will help you to understand any difficulties a child might be having and how you can help to overcome them.

Be guided by your SEN coordinator if you think you need to use these. The SEN coordinator will be able to guide you towards the best test. These are specific and need carrying out with close regard for the instructions that come with them if they are to be of any real value. Don't over-use them.

Evaluative assessments give information about aspects of the teaching.

The formative assessments you carry out should be discussed with your colleagues on a regular basis. As you plan the next week's work and activities take note of

- tasks that didn't allow the children to learn effectively
- tasks that inspired the children and caught their imaginations to take the learning further
- particular children who struggled with a new concept
- groups who worked well together.

This information can then be used to modify future planning or target work more precisely to those children who need something different.

Medium- and long-term plans can also be adjusted in the light of these discussions and the growing awareness of the needs and preferences of the children.

Assessment's place in the learning/teaching/planning cycle

Assessment is an integral part of the learning process, which in its simplest form can be shown as in Figure 1.

If you now qualify the 'teacher plans' to state 'teacher plans for the long term', 'teacher plans for the medium term' and 'teacher plans for the short term', you will see that assessment also needs to be qualified (Figures 2–4).

At each stage there will also be a degree of evaluative assessment happening, when you look at the impact your teaching had on the children's learning and take any action needed to modify your future planning and delivery.

At any stage you may need to carry out some diagnostic assessments to find out about particular children who are experiencing difficulties. Or there may be a whole-class problem – say, spelling is weak across all ability levels and you want to find out exactly where the children are at, developmentally, or where the problems are occurring, so that you can adapt your teaching input.

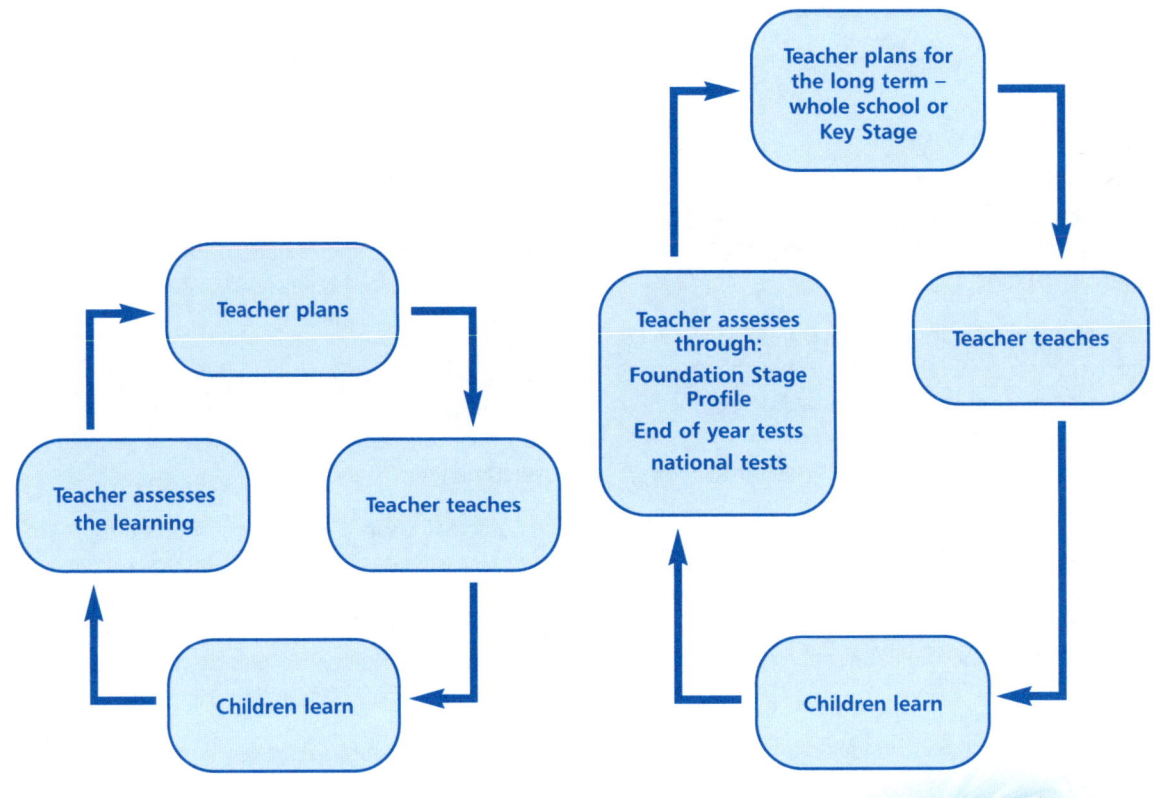

Figure 1

Teacher plans → Teacher teaches → Children learn → Teacher assesses the learning → (back to Teacher plans)

Figure 2

Teacher plans for the long term – whole school or Key Stage → Teacher teaches → Children learn → Teacher assesses through: Foundation Stage Profile, End of year tests, national tests → (back to Teacher plans for the long term)

The Assessment Handbook

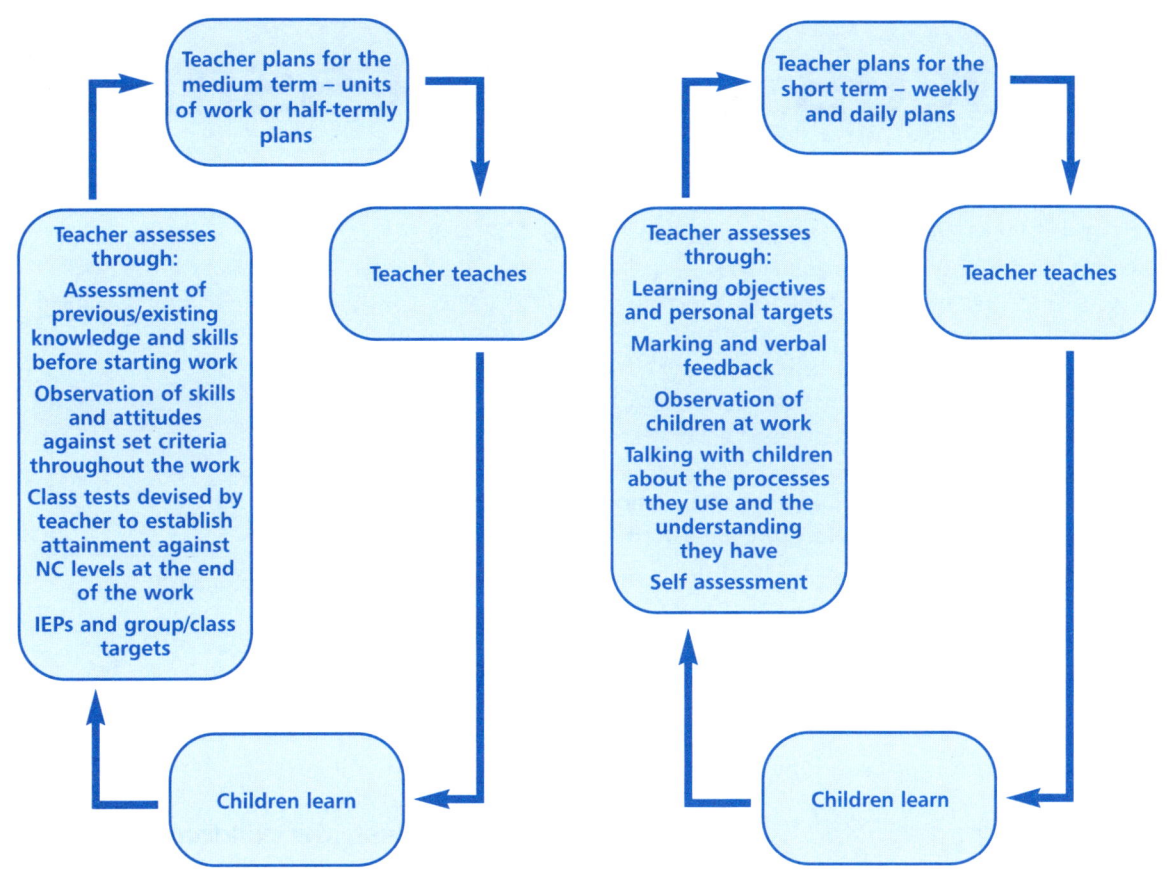

Figure 3

```
Teacher plans for the medium term – units of work or half-termly plans
  → Teacher teaches
    → Children learn
      → Teacher assesses through:
        • Assessment of previous/existing knowledge and skills before starting work
        • Observation of skills and attitudes against set criteria throughout the work
        • Class tests devised by teacher to establish attainment against NC levels at the end of the work
        • IEPs and group/class targets
```

Figure 4

```
Teacher plans for the short term – weekly and daily plans
  → Teacher teaches
    → Children learn
      → Teacher assesses through:
        • Learning objectives and personal targets
        • Marking and verbal feedback
        • Observation of children at work
        • Talking with children about the processes they use and the understanding they have
        • Self assessment
```

The school policy

'a policy is about action – it is not simply a set of beliefs. Reading a policy should give us some indication of what will be happening' (Skelton and Playfoot, 1995, p2)

The school policy for assessment will have been discussed and agreed by all members of staff and agreed with the governors. It will state the aims and objectives of assessment as defined within your school. For example,

> We aim to carry out assessments which will enable us to track the speed and level of development of individual pupils.

It will contain statements expressing your shared philosophy reflecting the ethos of your school. These statements will embody the action you take in the school. Policies are about reality, not aspirations, and should be a genuine reflection of what goes on in your school at this time. For example,

> We view assessment as the means to finding out how successful our teaching and the children's learning is. We modify our teaching plans in line with our findings.

Practical details will be broadly stated, to include timing, processes used for different types of assessment, and will identify the roles/names of those responsible for carrying it out. Examples of any record-keeping will be attached as appendices.

The policy should be reviewed frequently to make sure that it remains a true reflection of the assessments being carried out in the school.

It is your responsibility to read through any policy your school already has in place, and your role as a teacher to put that policy into action. You are the active part of the assessment policy and your teaching should show that you are responding to it.

> **Any assessments you carry out should always facilitate the children's learning.**

1 Focus on assessment

The term 'assessment' can cover tests and examinations, but it also encompasses all the other ways in which teachers monitor progress. The sort of assessment that merely gives you a grade tells you very little about which parts of the curriculum were understood and which parts were not. Equally, an assessment used to give a child's position within a class tells you very little except how that child compares with others. To be useful and meaningful, assessments need to be focused.

In this chapter there is information on

- how you can focus your assessments.

This chapter contains practical strategies for

- when you can gather the information
- how you can gather the information.

How you can focus your assessments

If assessment is to be a useful exercise it must always have a focus.

Why you are assessing the children

- To find out if the children have reached a particular target or learning objective, and to know where to take them to next (formative assessment).
- To provide a summary of what this cohort of children have achieved at this specific point in time, and to give you comparative data (summative assessment).
- To identify any area of weakness that is preventing the child from learning, and the possible response to it to enable the child to access learning (diagnostic assessment).
- To give you feedback on your teaching and the learning opportunities you are providing for your class so that you can amend your planning (evaluative assessment).

When to assess the children

- At the start of a unit of work, or even a specific lesson, to give you information about the level of the children's prior knowledge, onto which you will build the next layer of their learning.
- During an activity to give you information about how the children are approaching the work, which learning skills they are applying to their work, and the thought processes they are going through.
- At the end of a unit of work or lesson to give you information about the level of understanding the children have reached and any skills they have mastered. This will also guide your starting point for the next lesson or unit of work on this area of the curriculum.
- At key points throughout the child's time in school to give you information about the progress the child is making, or to inform you about the progress and comparative achievements of the whole cohort.

How to assess the children

- Observation.
- Questioning.
- Marking their work.
- Giving feedback.
- Engaging in dialogue with one or more of the children.
- Giving them a practical task to do, individually, in pairs or small groups.
- A pencil-and-paper exercise.
- A test, written or mental, your own or published.

You also need to decide on how you will record your findings and what you will do with the data the assessment gives you.

Always remember that the prime purpose of assessment is to help future learning. By knowing what children can and cannot do, you can plan for your children's future learning more effectively.

Gathering information

When?

- In the classroom in every lesson.

Assessment should be an ongoing activity in every teacher's classroom. It is the most powerful tool you possess and can be used at any time.

You are assessing children when you use questioning, when you are marking and as you observe them at work. This type of assessment is informal and you do it instinctively. Good teachers also use this method of assessment in a more structured way by planning their assessment opportunities as part of their general lesson planning.

When you identify assessment opportunities related to the learning objective of any lesson, you can determine the future needs of the children either individually, in groups or as a whole class and relate your future planned learning to what you have observed. For this type of assessment to be valuable, you must ensure clarity in the learning objective for the lesson. However, learning isn't always a straightforward step-by-step process and, sometimes, important learning takes place which you haven't planned for. Be prepared to recognise this and use it to aid your future planning.

How?

In the classroom, you are the major assessor of the children's work. Increasingly, though, the classroom teacher is supported by other adults working in the classroom. They also have excellent opportunities for gaining a detailed understanding of children's learning, especially as they are usually working with small groups with whom they have a close relationship, and they often have detailed knowledge of a child's strengths and weaknesses.

In order that they can understand their role in assessment, it is helpful to involve them in the planning for that group of children and also provide appropriate training in assessment.

> The Year 2 children were assessed by their teacher at the start of the year to find out exactly which phonic structures they knew in terms of spelling. She used a list of words which included each phoneme taught in the Literacy Strategy in Years 1 and 2. She gave a list of the phonemes in the order in which they would be taught, the lists of words in common usage, and the words needed for the numeracy lessons, to a highly experienced teaching assistant (TA). Together they grouped the children into five groups according to their spelling knowledge, and gave each child five or ten spellings to learn, according to their ability.
>
> At a fixed time on each day the TA took one of the groups, tested the spellings that they had been learning that week and gave them more spellings for the next week. If they knew all ten, they had ten new words. If a child only knew six then they were given six new words to add to the four they had yet to master. The TA chose spellings according to the needs of the curriculum taking into account the ability of the child.
>
> She recorded the number of correct spellings each week in an exercise book and adjusted the number of spellings (adding more or giving fewer) to keep the challenge achievable for the individual child.
>
> She reported back to the teacher when she was concerned or when she had made a change in the groupings. For example, Sam started off in a group of weak spellers but part-way through the spring term he suddenly grasped the idea of spelling and he was put in a group who had more, and harder, words each week. He was so proud of his achievement. When a small group were noticed to be making little progress because they had no help at home, the TA did daily practice with them in the few moments when the class was tidying up, or getting ready for play or PE.

Increasingly, children are becoming involved in their own assessments, as active rather than passive learners. Again, it is important that learning objectives are made explicit. Children need to be guided as to what they are learning and when they have achieved it.

The Year 4 teacher has a whiteboard in her room, on which she writes each of the learning objectives for the day. At the start of each lesson she adds the specific intentions for that lesson to the list on the board and talks about it with the children, making sure that they understand what it means in practical terms. By the end of the day there will be four or five learning objectives listed there.

At the end of the day she goes through the list with the children and they award themselves a grade, as follows.

- I feel really confident about this. I know it. **5 points**
- I'm nearly there. If we do it again once more, then I think I'll know it. **3 points**
- I'm not at all sure about this. I would like to do some more work on it. **1 point**

The children total their own points for the day.

As they talk, the teacher can see where uncertainty lies – even though children may have completed the task she set them and they seem to have understood, the general feeling seems to be that they would like more work on this. The children don't feel secure in their knowledge. The teacher can adapt her plans to allow a little more time on this.

Assessment in the classroom often takes the form of differentiated questioning and discussion, which seeks to bring out a child's understanding of the learning objective. Observation by the teacher is another important skill that can be utilised. Marking is the obvious form of assessment and is much more successful if interactive. This could mean that the child is present when the work is marked. This can prove difficult with a large class but can be done on a rota basis so that each child receives quality feedback at regular intervals. Another way this can be done is by allowing children to answer written comments on their work so that a dialogue takes place. Children's self-assessment is another powerful tool allowing the child some 'thinking time' to reflect on their work or allowing them time to share it with their peers, either in a one-to-one situation or with the whole class. (You will find out more about each of these methods in later chapters of this handbook.)

When?

- Ongoing assessment over a period of time.

This is a collection of daily or weekly assessments combined to provide an overview of a child's progress. These assessments may be informal, such as notes in a teacher's book, or more formal notes kept in relation to a child's individual education plan. (There are more ideas for doing this in Chapter 4 of this handbook.)

Don't attempt to keep all of the children's work for this. It can be done in their everyday exercise books for the most part. You only need to keep a record of the outcomes. You could devise spreadsheets on a program such as Excel™, which will allow you to manipulate the figures and collate your information. Or stick to an old-fashioned but accessible and easy-to-use squared-paper exercise book.

These ongoing assessments should be used to support future planned work and shared with other staff in the classroom.

How?

You may decide to carry out a five-minute mental maths test with your children every Friday at the start of your numeracy lesson for that day. The children could keep a personal record of their score or you could have a class list.

You may choose to have a separate exercise book in which the children do a piece of unaided writing – fiction or non-fiction – once every half-term. Annotate it with your comments, the child's levels of achievement and their next target. Before the children start their writing they should read through the comments from the previous piece and try to respond to the set targets.

Individual targets for children can be set from these ongoing assessments, providing a series of things to work towards. The children can take responsibility for these targets and also responsibility for showing the teacher that they have achieved it.

In a small junior school, the children have personal target cards. The teachers have prepared a list of numbered steps towards the goals they need to achieve in literacy and numeracy over the year. They are placed where the children can see them. These targets are written in child-friendly language.

- I can write stories that keep the reader interested.
- I can use question marks properly.
- I can add three one-digit numbers together in my head.

They need to be small, challenging and easily measurable.

Together with the teacher, the child sets his or her targets in literacy and numeracy, referring to the teacher's list. Targets for behaviour, concentration and so on, can be added if that is necessary for an individual child. Children keep the cards and record their personal goals and when they have achieved them. There is no greater way to success than increased self-esteem!

When?

- Block assessments.

Often in schools the learning is planned into units of work, again with assessment opportunities built into the planning. For this to happen effectively, the medium- and short-term plans have to have clearly identified learning objectives. You will then be able to assess children's prior knowledge at the start of the unit of work, monitor their progress and assess their learning skills throughout the work and carry out another assessment at, or towards the end of, the unit to check on the children's attainments and understanding. This will also feed into your future planning for these children and may affect the way that you present the work to future groups.

One consideration with regard to block assessments is 'When is the best time to do them?'. You may want to consider assessing before the end of a unit so that weaknesses can be addressed.

How?

Assessment first needs to take place at the beginning of a block of work to enable the teacher to match the topic as closely as possible to the children's needs. If best use of these findings is to be made, the medium-term planning needs to be flexible.

When introducing a unit of work on 'Our Village' to her Year 1 class, the teacher showed the children a large aerial photograph of the centre of the village. Immediately the children started to point out landmarks, and identify buildings. As they did this, the teacher wrote the name of each building on a sheet of A4 paper and pinned it up near the photograph. In response to her questioning and within the general discussion, the children offered much more information, which was written onto the appropriate sheet of paper.

'The church is really, really old.' 'My grandad went to that church.' 'The scout hut's made out of wood.' 'My sister goes to Brownies in the scout hut.' 'That's where the babies go to playgroup.' 'If you look round the back of the shop you can see where the swings used to be.'

Each of the completed sheets gives the teacher an indication of what the children already know about their village. It gives her some useful areas for further investigation – Why are the swings no longer there? It sets up scenes for the children to link to, to make their learning more meaningful – What did the village look like when your Grandad went to the church as a little boy? Which buildings were still there? Which ones have changed?

Throughout the unit of work you will be assessing progress through your observations of the skills the children use, the way that they tackle the tasks you have set them, their ability to research material and solve problems. You will be noting their responses to the questions you are asking them. You can set up a dialogue with a group of children and find out how much they understand. As you mark the children's work you can check their understanding and offer them feedback on how they are doing, guiding them to the next aspect they need to think about.

Assessments are then usually made after the work is completed for a particular block. It isn't necessary to use a formal test for assessing understanding although you may decide to ask the children to complete a written test. It can be just as informative to use careful questioning, discussion, observation and marking. The important thing to note is that the assessment is planned for and systematic in order to get a good picture of a child's abilities.

> At the start of a unit of science on natural materials, the Year 5 class were shown a picture of an outcrop of rocks in a wild and natural landscape. They were then each given a large sheet of paper (flipchart size), onto which they were invited to stick or draw pictures, and add labels, words and phrases to show how much they already knew about such natural materials. They set up subsections of knowledge on the characteristics and properties of these materials. All the written work was in one colour. The teacher collected these in and used them to assess the children's prior knowledge.
>
> Towards the end of the unit they were handed back to the children. Using a different coloured pen they added new information and crossed out any mis-information. It was easy for them to see how far they had come. Their knowledge was greatly expanded and the proof was in front of them.

One of the ways you can assess the children is through their performance. Start by formulating the outcomes that you want to measure, at both the cognitive and affective levels. Design a task (role-plays, experiments, discussions) that will allow the children to use the skills, behaviours or performance you want to measure. The task should be complex, allowing you to assess a variety of skills, and does not necessarily have to lead to one particular 'right' outcome. It should also be sufficiently representative to allow you to make generalisations about the skills being assessed.

Develop a standard procedure for presenting the task to the children, and a scoring rubric that clearly lists the elements you want to assess, such as attitudes, skills and cognitive processes. If you are assessing clearly observable behaviour, draw up a checklist on which you can note whether the behaviour has or has not occurred. This can be very useful when providing feedback to the children.

Once devised, any test or task used for assessment can become part of the resources for that topic. Make sure that you label it clearly with the learning intentions which it was designed to check. The advantage of designing your own tests is that they can be accurately matched to the learning objectives in your classroom, not just parts of them. Try to make these tests able to assess differing types of knowledge such as factual, procedural and thinking skills. Use a variety of testing methods such as multiple-choice or open questions. Use tests diagnostically and provide children with feedback.

This will allow you to integrate assessment with teaching by identifying weaknesses and teaching to overcome them.

Across the year group or the whole school you can build a portfolio of material showing success at each level – 'This is what a piece of writing at Level 2a looks like. It shows evidence of…' – which can then be used to aid future assessment.

Children's self-evaluation of a block of work is also a good method of assessment. Here the children can assess their work against certain criteria and develop their own skills of target-setting.

A simple format to use is to create a sheet with the sub-headings

- All about …
- New things I know
- New things I can do
- Things I would like to find out more about
- Things I need to keep practising.

This can be distributed at the end of each unit of work, completed and then stuck into the child's exercise book.

When?

- Year-end assessments.

Most schools now use some form of year-end assessment. QCA produce optional English and maths tests which provide a useful way of checking and monitoring work through Key Stage 2. This also provides children with opportunities to become familiar with the style of test they will encounter at the end of the key stage.

How?

The formal tests produced by QCA are useful because they give you comparative data year on year, in addition to checking the progress for an individual child.

You can use published tests for spelling, reading and maths, which will give you standardised results, and in some instances can be translated into quotients, which are a more informative way of monitoring progress.

You can devise tests within your own school which you repeat each year. This can be a time-consuming activity. You must be sure that they will give you the information you want and that they allow the children the opportunity to share their knowledge, understanding and skills as appropriate.

The Assessment Handbook

Each half-term throughout the year the class covered one unit of work from the science curriculum, and at points within each unit the children had a worksheet to complete. The teacher decided to choose one sheet from each unit of work, and clip them together to make six-page booklets. The children were then given this towards the end of the school year. They could take as long as they needed to work through the six activities again, all equipment was available to them, but they had to do the work unaided and totally independently (there was help with reading any questions for the weak readers). This gave the teacher the chance to find out who had retained the learning, who had improved, and who had forgotten or still couldn't do the task. Children could show their ability to find the right equipment for the task.

This was a time-saver for the teacher as the sheets had already been created and the learning objectives were stated on them. The children approached them with confidence, recognising the activities and taking on the challenge to 'do it better than last time'.

When?

- End of key stage assessment.

Assessment at the end of each key stage is directed by law. The requirements for the assessment and recording arrangements are published annually for Key Stage 1 and Key Stage 2 in booklets from the QCA. Care needs to be taken that you carry these out in strict conformity with the regulations. You need to prepare the children for these so that they are familiar with the format, but not daunted by the experience.

When?

- Foundation Stage Profile.

The Foundation Stage Profile replaces statutory baseline assessment on entry to primary school and with it comes a recognition that throughout the Foundation Stage assessment plays an important role in each child's development. The profile recognises the need for well-planned observations in providing reliable assessment information and by the end of the Foundation Stage should summarise a child's achievements, providing valuable information for teachers in schools.

How?

One major change in the collection of evidence is that the teacher is expected to involve many other people, including

- anyone in the school who has dealings with the child – teaching assistants, lunchtime supervisors and so on
- parents
- pre-school providers
- other professionals – specialist teachers, therapists and so on
- the children themselves.

When the teacher writes the profile she is taking all of these points of view into account to give a rounded picture of the child.

So remember…

1. The prime purpose of assessment is to help future learning, which means that something must happen as a result of the assessment.

2. Focus your assessment so that you know why you will carry it out. Assessment opportunities have been grouped into different categories such as summative, formative, diagnostic and evaluative. Each has its place and one of the teacher's many skills is to know when to use each one.

3. Plan the most appropriate time to carry out any specific assessment.

4. Build assessment opportunities into your planning.

5. Think about how you will carry out the assessment. There are different kinds of assessment we can use when making decisions about children's learning.

6. The reason we assess children is to check whether they have achieved the learning objectives we have set.

7. Assessment is a shared process.

2 Learning styles

Understanding how the children in your class learn can help you to plan your assessments in such a way that you can give every child the opportunity to show the breadth and depth of their learning. Understanding your own preferred style can help you to evaluate your own teaching.

In this chapter there is information on

- what we mean by the term 'learning styles'
- why you need to know about learning styles
- how to broaden your own teaching and learning styles
- how you can recognise children's learning styles.

This chapter contains practical strategies for

- assessing your children's preferred learning styles
- considering learning styles when planning and teaching
- developing children's less dominant learning styles.

What we mean by the term 'learning styles'

A learning style is the way in which we perceive, understand, organise and recall information. Researchers agree that learning styles can be distinguished, but the way that they are defined is open to debate. Learning style models are based on different schools of thought. Some of the most well known are listed here.

1. **Information-processing models** – these refer to the way that our brains process information. They include

    - the first part of Kolb's experiential learning cycle, describing the processes of learning
    - Gardner's theory of multiple intelligences, which refers to the way that we use our abilities to process information (see below)
    - Gregoric mind styles – this model shows that people have relative strengths sorted as abstract-sequential, abstract-random, concrete-sequential and concrete-random, and individuals may have various combinations of these strengths or even a balance of all four.

2. **Personality models** – these refer to the way we interact with our environment. It is thought that our preferred learning styles are influenced by our previous learning experiences, genetic make-up, environment and culture. These models include

    - the second part of Kolb's experiential learning cycle describing individual learning styles
    - Gardner's theory of multiple intelligences – each individual has different abilities in eight areas (linguistic, logical/mathematical, musical, bodily/kinaesthetic, visual/spatial, naturalistic, interpersonal, intrapersonal)
    - Myers–Briggs type indicator – a revision of Carl Jung's categorisation of types of people
    - McCarthy's four learning styles describing children as innovative learners, analytic learners, common-sense learners or dynamic learners.

3. **Perceptual modality** – this refers to the way that we take in information using the senses. The most well-known model is

    - VAK (visual, auditory, kinaesthetic) – this model is used in the accelerated learning approach.

'Accelerated learning' covers a number of theoretical and practical approaches to teaching and learning. These have been developed as a result of research into how the brain works and an improved understanding of how we learn. The accelerated learning approach encompasses a belief that all learners can reach a level of achievement that may seem beyond them. In order to do this they need to be taught effectively within a supportive learning environment and be given opportunities to understand and use their preferred learning styles.

This chapter will use the VAK model to discuss the implications of considering both teaching and learning styles in your classroom.

Why you need to know about learning styles

Sandra Rief (1993) states that children retain 10% of what they read, 20% of what they hear, 30% of what they see, 50% of what they see and hear, 70% of what they say, and 90% of what they say and do.

We can see from this statement that children are constantly processing information through their senses. Different children rely on each of the senses to varying degrees. Most children have a preference for one or more modes of learning and this constitutes their preferred learning style. Some children have a dominant learning style and have difficulty accessing information unless they are able to use this style. If children are given opportunities to learn using their strengths then they are more successful. They tend to learn in a more natural way, making their learning easier and more enjoyable.

As teachers we need to be aware that we should vary our teaching style in order to accommodate the learning needs of all our children. Sometimes we need to present information using a balance of teaching styles, in order to allow learners to experience not only their own preferred learning style but to be able to collaborate with other learners who have different learning styles. Sometimes, despite our best efforts to ensure variety in the way that we present information, our children still experience difficulty in grasping certain concepts.

> A mixed ability Year 6 class had been studying water and its effect on landscapes and people. They had followed the course of a nearby river for about half a mile and, with adult prompting, had noted some of its effect on the environment. Back at school, visual material, in the form of maps, photographs, diagrams and drawings had been put on display. However, despite the environmental visit and the use of visual materials, the teacher found that many of the children did not fully understand the meaning of some of the key vocabulary. He decided to take the class outside where he asked them to gather materials that could represent natural features such as rocks, trees and soil. In small groups the children then arranged these materials on the sloping part of their playground. Each group had a container of water as the source of their 'river'. The children were asked to observe what happened when the water encountered each type of natural feature. They then had to explain this in their own words. Back in the classroom the teacher asked the children to match some of the key vocabulary to their own explanations. Later one boy was heard to explain to a friend, 'I think our river eroded more soil than yours because we made our water go quicker'.

We can see from this example that a number of children in the class had kinaesthetic/tactile strengths. They needed a 'hands-on' approach to help them understand the key conceptual vocabulary linked to this project.

How to broaden your own teaching/learning style

As teachers, we all have our own preferred learning styles and these influence the way that we teach. Sometimes this means that we continue to use a narrow and defined range of teaching strategies because they feel safe and familiar. Often we feel that if these strategies have been successful then there should be no need to change.

However, if we really wish to find the most stimulating ways of teaching then we need to be prepared to broaden our own teaching and learning styles in order to accommodate children's learning styles. This means that we may need to

- evaluate our current teaching and learning styles
- investigate a range of different teaching strategies and techniques
- share recognised ideas on good practice
- explore ways of involving the children in taking control of their own learning.

Observing other teachers' lessons and noting the different strategies and techniques employed by them, can act as a starting point when evaluating our own teaching and learning styles. We also need to be prepared to investigate different teaching strategies and techniques by attending courses, reading up-to-date educational material, visiting other schools and sharing ideas with colleagues. In this way we can broaden our thinking and incorporate new ideas into our teaching.

The Assessment Handbook

> Mrs G was a charismatic teacher. She had the ability to hold a group, class or whole school in the palm of her hand. She was the deputy headteacher and had the respect of everyone in the school. She was able to read a poem or teach a new maths concept with similar dramatic effect.
>
> However, observations made by a visiting advisor suggested that she needed to vary her teaching style in order to accommodate the children's different learning styles.
>
> Mrs G was given the opportunity to visit other schools where she could observe a variety of teaching strategies and techniques and reflect on different teaching and learning styles. She shared her findings with the staff at her own school and together they began to evaluate their own teaching and learning styles as well as those of their children. They then set up a teaching and learning group whose brief was to
>
> - share recognised ideas on good practice
> - investigate different teaching strategies and techniques
> - explore ways of involving the children in taking control of their own learning.
>
> Mrs G introduced the idea of 'preferred learning styles' to the children in her class. They were keen to identify their strengths and be given opportunities to use these strengths in their own learning.

At the end of any week, you could analyse the tasks and activities you set for the children. Which of the three learning styles (VAK) did you use? Was there a balance or did your own preferred style dominate? As you plan for next week, try to plan tasks that will engage all of the children, allowing them to use their different senses.

How you can recognise children's learning styles

Gardner's theory of multiple intelligences claims that everyone has different abilities in each of eight areas. Traditional education has tended to favour the linguistic and logical-mathematical areas with a greater emphasis placed on being able to listen, understand and recall information in these areas. Many children have difficulty coping with traditional teaching styles and need to experience a wider range of learning experiences that help them to develop their strengths while at the same time strengthening their weaknesses.

The best way of recognising the learning styles of the children in your class is by observing their learning behaviour. You need to organise open-ended activities that allow them a choice of responses. They will usually choose to respond by using their preferred learning style. These are some of the most common recognisable characteristics of children with different learning styles.

Visual learners like to learn through written language and visual/spatial materials. They like to

- use diagrams, graphs, maps and charts
- relate text to illustrations
- design posters and draw pictures to convey information
- use mind maps to help them organise information
- use cue cards and prompt sheets
- refer to wall charts and visual organisers
- use visual memory spelling techniques
- use visualisation techniques for story-writing
- use scanning techniques in reading.

Auditory/aural learners like to learn by listening and talking. They like to

- take an active part in guided group reading activities
- share their ideas in circletime
- play language and word games
- take part in role-play and drama
- take an active part in collaborative group work
- talk about their written work
- join in saying aloud rhymes, chants and performance poetry
- take part in auditory discrimination games and activities
- enjoy giving talks and presentations
- take an active part in discussions, debates and interviews.

A Year 3 class teacher was trying to encourage her children to take risks in their learning. She explained that everyone learns in a different way and makes different responses to tasks.

As part of an open-ended activity the teacher read the fable 'The crow and the water jug' to her class. She left the story unfinished and asked the children to talk with a partner about the crow's problem. She then asked each pair to think of a way to explain how the crow managed to get a drink of water from the tall jug. She emphasised that the children could use any of the tools and materials that were available in the classroom to help them with their explanation.

The majority of the children drew a picture or a diagram to explain their solution to the crow's problem. Some used role-play to enact the ending of the story. Two children chose to retell the story adding their own ending and two children chose to demonstrate their solution. They used a plastic jug with a small amount of water at the bottom and modelling clay formed in the shape of stones. The rest of the class were fascinated by this demonstration and everyone wanted to try out the solution for themselves.

The teacher was delighted with the range of children's responses and was able to recognise some of the children's preferred learning styles through this open-ended activity.

Kinaesthetic/tactile learners like to learn through movement and touch. They like to

- have regular 'brain break' activities interspersed between their learning
- use whiteboards and highlighter pens
- use magnetic numbers and letters for support with literacy and numeracy
- enjoy action games and rhymes
- take an active part in IT control activities
- enjoy modelling using a range of tools and media
- take an active part in movement and mime
- play language and word games
- learn through practical/concrete activities
- enjoy active learning, eg. clapping syllables when spelling, skipping when reciting times tables.

Assessing your children's preferred learning styles

There are a number of learning styles inventories and questionnaires available on the Internet. The Alps Approach Resource Book (*Accelerated Learning in the Primary School*) has a photocopiable learning preference questionnaire that you could give to your children. While child-friendly questionnaires can help to raise your and your children's awareness of their preferred learning style, it is also important that you set up systems for ongoing teacher assessment of children's strengths and weaknesses. A variety of focused tasks can be identified and incorporated into normal classroom teaching. If the main focus of the activity is auditory then you can assess the level of success achieved by your children in this area and build up a profile for each child. This may sound complex but it is actually quite simple and can form part of your ongoing teacher assessment (see example overleaf).

This example shows children being assessed, in groups of six, while taking part in focused activities related to different areas of the curriculum. For instance, you could ask your children to create a mind map in several different lessons, giving you the opportunity to assess them in more than one situation.

The scoring system rates the level of success achieved by the child for each activity.

Score 1 – Experiences difficulties even with support.

Score 2 – Fairly successful with guidance.

Score 3 – Successful, independent learner.

An analysis of this assessment shows that five of the children in this group have kinaesthetic strengths (see page 19). It is important that they are given opportunities to use these strengths across the curriculum. The assessment also shows that three children have difficulties with using a visual learning style. They will need to be given support in developing their less dominant learning styles.

Children do not fall neatly into specific types of learners. Instead they tend to have specific learning strengths with some being more helpful than others in particular learning situations. For instance, RG has visual strengths that help her when designing and making a puppet but are not so helpful when she is involved in a mime activity. She clearly needs support with developing her gross motor skills.

Tasks	ML	SA	RG	SB	GR	AF
Visual Design a poster	3	1	3	1	2	1
Create a mind map	2	1	3	1	2	1
Auditory Listen to a story/recall main points	2	2	2	2	3	1
20 questions about an artefact	2	1	2	2	3	1
Kinaesthetic Make a finger puppet	3	2	3	1	2	2
Mime an everyday situation	3	3	1	3	1	3

The Assessment Handbook

Considering learning styles when planning and teaching

'If you think there is only one answer, then you will only find one.'
(Scottish CCC, 1996)

We need to be aware of the multi-faceted aspects of our role and the effect that our teaching style has on our children. Self-awareness and self-esteem, coupled with physical and emotional well-being, are important elements of effective learning and give children the confidence to try different ways of solving problems, exploring ideas and learning new skills. We should be providing opportunities for children to develop their individual gifts by employing effective teaching methods.

Research into what makes an effective teacher has begun to recognise that this is also true of teachers. Recently researchers have begun

'…to identify more systematically what teachers, who are considered to be good at their job, actually do in the classroom. The intention has been to see if we can go beyond lists of skills and qualities to understanding how effective teachers operate.'
(Scottish CCC, 1996)

The Scottish CCC, in their consultation paper, identified nine ways in which effective teachers operate. Two of these refer to the recognition of preferred teaching and learning styles. Effective teachers realise that they cannot provide individual teaching but tend to present a range of learning experiences that enable their children to use their preferred learning styles.

By using a multi-sensory teaching approach you can present information in a combination of ways. You can vary the mode of presentation throughout each lesson. In this way you can provide a variety of stimuli that will appeal to all learners. When creating a multi-sensory environment you should ensure that you have a range of materials and activities available.

In order to stimulate the visual sense you need to

- provide visual displays (wall charts, pictures, photographs, maps, diagrams, flowcharts, posters, mind maps) relating to the lesson
- help your children to develop colour coding systems to put information into categories or to highlight key facts
- encourage your children to use alternative methods of recording (writing frames, diagrams, labelled pictures, flowcharts, word webs, maps) as well as narrative and non-narrative writing
- ensure that your children make effective use of the computer for organising and presenting their work
- make flashcards for key vocabulary or information – you can draw symbols, pictures or colour-code the cards to help your children remember the information
- use visualisation techniques when introducing a subject or asking children to write a story.

In order to stimulate the auditory/aural sense you need to

- use audio tapes and videos
- encourage collaborative group work particularly during investigation and problem-solving activities
- provide opportunities for role-play and drama activities
- allow children to 'rehearse' their learning by using the technique of 'think, pair, share'
- help children develop their literacy skills through language and word games and their numeracy skills through number concept games
- incorporate speaking and listening activities (interviews, twenty questions, guest speakers, hot-seating, debates) into your lessons.

In order to stimulate the kinaesthetic/tactile sense you need to

- provide regular 'brain breaks' interspersed between learning sessions
- ensure that whiteboards, magnetic boards and highlighter pens are readily available
- help children develop their investigation and problem-solving skills through practical/concrete experiences
- use the environment as an extended classroom (field trips, learning centres, nature trails, history walks)
- provide opportunities for movement and mime to be incorporated into your lessons
- use IT control activities, board games, demonstrations, constructional apparatus and a variety of tools and media in your lessons.

A Year 5 mixed ability class had been studying aspects of change in the local area with a particular focus on housing. As part of their project they were taken on a walk around the area near their school. The teacher asked them to be history detectives and record detailed observations about the different types of houses in the area. The children were encouraged to use alternative methods of recording (labelled pictures, diagrams, sketches, maps) as well as written notes. Some of the children were given the responsibility of taking photographs using a digital camera.

On returning to the classroom the children were asked to create mind maps in order to help them organise their observations into categories. Pictures, diagrams, sketches and photographs were put on display and the children were asked to use a range of information sources to help them date the houses they had seen. Follow-up lessons involved the children working in small groups to investigate changes, over time, in architectural styles, window shapes, building materials, etc. Each group was then asked to give an illustrated talk on their findings.

Developing children's less dominant learning styles

If we use a multi-sensory teaching approach, our children will experience learning by using both their preferred learning styles and their less dominant learning styles during our lessons. For some children this may present few difficulties as they can adapt and apply different ways of learning to a task. Other children may be less adaptable and may have difficulty accessing information unless they are able to use their dominant learning style. In order to help our children develop their less dominant learning styles we need to ensure that the activities we offer are well differentiated and fun. It is important that we give all children opportunities not only to use their strengths, but also to strengthen their weaknesses. We need to do this in a way that enhances our children's self-esteem and builds their confidence.

Talk with the children about the different ways in which people learn. Help them to identify their own strengths and talk with them about activities that could help them to improve other aspects.

'Differentiation of learning activities within the primary curriculum framework will help schools to meet the learning needs of all children … Schools should not assume that children's learning difficulties always result solely, or even mainly, from problems within the child. A school's own practices make a difference – for good or ill.'
(DfES, 2001, 6:18)

Activities to strengthen the visual sense could include

- spot the difference – searching for visual similarities and differences in words and pictures
- word searches – scanning
- visual memory spelling games – using the look, cover, remember, write, check strategy with high frequency words
- Pelmanism – shapes, symbols, pictures, words
- tessellation activities
- ten ways to describe a chair – this could be any object related to the subject of the lesson
- computer-aided picture and design activities
- what happens next? – pictorial prediction.

Activities to strengthen the auditory sense could include

- same/different – identifying rhyming and non-rhyming words
- sound walk – identifying specific sounds in the environment
- circletime
- story tapes and comprehension activities
- twenty questions – allow children twenty questions to discover the identity of a hidden object related to a class project – they need to listen carefully to make deductions
- hot-seating – children compose questions to ask the person in the 'hot seat' – this could be a visitor or an adult or child taking on the role of a story character or a famous person from history.

Activities to strengthen the kinaesthetic/tactile sense could include

- movement games requiring children to use space and position

- map directions – following and giving directions using a map or plan related to a class project
- brain gym
- puppetry – link to class project
- clay modelling – link to class project
- design and technology projects.

Most of the activities can be incorporated into literacy and numeracy hours, or other areas of the curriculum. All children should be given as many opportunities as possible to transfer and generalise the skills they learn in order to ensure that the skills remain in their long-term memory.

> A group of Year 2 children with learning difficulties had been using digit cards to play a variety of number games. All these games related to numbers up to 20. Most of the children in the group had difficulty writing the 'teen' numbers and frequently reversed the digit order. Using the digit cards during each mental/oral session helped to strengthen the children's kinaesthetic/tactile senses and they soon became more confident with understanding digit order in numbers up to 50. The children were then asked to use their digit cards to investigate the features of odd and even numbers to 50. They discovered that the last digit in a two-digit number gave them a clue. Each child in the group was able to explain why a certain number was odd or even and give evidence from the investigation. During the next session some of the children were able to extend their knowledge by using both two- and three-digit numbers. During this session it became obvious that one of the children in the group was particularly gifted in the area of numeracy and was able to use his ability in more complex investigations.

We can see from this example that one child's exceptional ability had been masked by his difficulties with accessing the curriculum through visual and auditory learning strategies. Because the children in the group had language difficulties, the teacher had been careful to provide plenty of visual stimulus. However, it was not until she employed kinaesthetic/tactile teaching strategies that this child's abilities became evident.

So remember...

1 Children are constantly processing information through their senses.

2 Different children rely on each of the senses to varying degrees.

3 Most children have a preference for one or more modes of learning and this constitutes their preferred learning style.

4 Some children have a 'dominant learning style' and have difficulty accessing information unless they are able to use this style.

5 Evaluate your own current teaching and learning styles and consider how far you are meeting the learning needs of your children.

6 Investigate different teaching strategies and techniques, to help you vary your teaching style, in order to accommodate the learning needs of all your children.

7 The best way of recognising the learning styles of the children in your class is by observing their learning behaviour.

8 Set up ongoing teacher assessment of your children's learning strengths and weaknesses.

9 Using a multi-sensory teaching approach can help you present information in a combination of ways.

10 Develop children's less dominant learning styles through well-differentiated, fun activities.

The Assessment Handbook

3 Tracking progress

Tracking progress is about gathering individual information about children, on a regular basis, and then sharing that information with all those involved with the education of those children. The information should give the children, parents, teachers and LEAs regular opportunities to analyse, evaluate and reflect on the educational needs of individuals, groups and cohorts.

In this chapter there is information on

- why you need to track children's progress
- how to track children's progress
- how to use the data gathered from tracking progress
- how you can link tracking progress to target-setting.

This chapter contains practical strategies for

- tracking children's progress beyond the core curriculum
- tracking development in literacy and numeracy
- linking tracking progress to target setting
- effective teacher intervention
- tracking gifted and SEN children.

Why you need to track children's progress

It is important to track children's progress for a number of reasons.

1. Identifying strengths and weaknesses of individuals, groups and cohorts. This helps to highlight specific educational needs such as those of SEN, gifted and talented, Traveller children, etc.

2. Checking progress of individuals, groups and cohorts against prior attainment. This helps everyone to view progress within realistic contexts.

3. Providing information for target-setting. Information gathered helps when setting individual SMART targets as well as group and cohort targets.

4. Providing information to support the monitoring and reviewing of targets set. Continuous assessment allows everyone to review progress alongside targets. Children can be motivated when they see that they are making progress towards their targets.

5. Monitoring the effectiveness of teaching and learning. Formative assessment allows teachers to evaluate the effectiveness of their teaching at regular intervals. It also provides information that can be used by headteachers to monitor effective teaching and learning in the school.

6. Informing curriculum planning. The specific educational needs that have been highlighted by tracking children's progress can be addressed through differentiated curriculum planning.

7. Providing information on transition from one year group to another and across school phases. It is important that children are not left to 'mark time' while new teachers assess their abilities.

8. Comparing attainment of individuals, groups and cohorts against local and national standards. You need to view your children's progress within a wider perspective.

9. Accountability – providing evidence of progress for external agencies, LEAs and Ofsted.

How to track children's progress

As teachers you collect a wide variety of information about the children you teach. This information may range from facts such as date of birth, position in family to a detailed diagnosis of an individual's special educational needs. In order to track children's progress effectively it is important to have an efficient central IT recording system on which the vast majority of the information can be collected and collated. You then need to decide, within a whole-school framework, the different ways in which you are going to gather the information that will help you track progress. You will probably use summative, formative and diagnostic assessment.

Summative assessments provide specific test results. These results show performance levels in specific subjects, by individual children, on a given day under test conditions. Summative assessments can include

- baseline assessments
- Foundation Stage Profile
- P Scale performance descriptors
- Key Stage 1 and Key Stage 2 national tests
- QCA optional tests at Years 3, 4 and 5
- standardised reading and spelling tests
- published maths tests.

Formative assessments are used by teachers to gain an understanding of what children know or have not understood about a specific area of learning or unit of work. This type of assessment should be linked to your teaching and learning practices. The information gained should help you to respond, and adapt your teaching to your children's educational needs. Feedback is an important element of formative assessment. It should include suggestions for improvement as well as encouraging children to focus on developing their understanding of skills and concepts rather than on giving limited answers. When taking part in formative assessment tasks children need to understand the learning objectives and the assessment criteria associated with the task. Formative assessments can include

- individual portfolios of work, compiled regularly and annotated
- end of unit tasks or tests in subject schemes of work
- problem-solving and investigation tasks – observations of children's responses recorded
- class discussion using open-ended questioning techniques – specific responses noted
- compositional writing tasks – criteria for assessment shared with children
- open-ended homework tasks followed by think, pair, share discussion – specific responses noted
- marking and oral/written feedback on children's everyday work.

Diagnostic assessment involves using tests that are criterion-referenced. This means that the test items are determined according to fixed criteria. Such tests are designed to evaluate children's strengths and weaknesses and provide information about individual educational needs. These tests are usually carried out in an individual or small-group setting.

Diagnostic assessments can include

- cognitive ability tests
- non-verbal reasoning tests
- screening tests for specific learning difficulties
- miscue analysis/running records
- published reading and spelling tests
- published maths tests.

How you decide to track progress will depend on the needs of the children in your school and should form part of your policy for assessment.

Staff at a village school, with 143 children on role, were concerned because both their Key Stage 1 and Key Stage 2 national test results were poor. They decided to investigate possible reasons by a careful examination of the areas of difficulty experienced by the children in the tests. Activities were set up in the classrooms that included the areas of difficulty identified. It soon became apparent that the children could not attempt some activities because of their limited understanding of the vocabulary used.

The staff decided to screen the children for understanding of vocabulary on entry to the school using BPVS (British Picture Vocabulary Scales). They used the information gained from this data to set up a comprehensive system of vocabulary support in Key Stage 1. This included using adults to ensure understanding of vocabulary in guided role-play situations, practical maths activities (conceptual vocabulary), guided group reading activities (specific vocabulary comprehension in context) and practical science activities (conceptual vocabulary).

The staff also decided to use a standardised reading test at the end of Year 1 and the end of Year 2. They chose the Primary Reading Test because it tested reading and understanding. It could be used with a whole year group and parallel forms allowed for year on year comparison of data.

At the end of the first year, Key Stage 1 national test results showed some improvement. Staff decided to introduce a similar tracking system at Key Stage 2 as well as setting up a system of vocabulary support. This included the introduction of visual cues for conceptual vocabulary in specific areas of the curriculum as well as teaching the children how to transfer their understanding of this vocabulary into other areas of the curriculum.

Tracking children's progress beyond the core curriculum

Tracking progress is not just about collecting information about children's knowledge, skills and concepts in academic subjects. It is also about helping them to develop their individuality and to mature as people, and keeping a record of this development.

Your mixed ability classes often reflect a real cross-section of the community, and within your classroom community you can observe how your children interact with each other. You can provide opportunities for your children to grow in social and emotional maturity and develop their personalities.

Some formative assessment tasks are useful because they allow you to make observations about children that are not necessarily related to their academic achievements. It is important that these observations are noted and shared with the children so that they can appreciate the progress they are making in all areas of their lives. It is also important that this progress is charted as it may reveal significant changes in a child's rate of development that need to be investigated. You may notice a gifted child underachieving or a child with learning difficulties displaying unexpected skills.

You also have to cater for a wide range of educational needs in mixed ability classes. These needs can range from severe learning difficulties to children who have high ability in specific areas of the curriculum. In order to be able to track the progress of children of all levels of ability you need to use a range of strategies and techniques that will give your children opportunities to develop their strengths and strengthen their weaknesses.

Teaching strategies and techniques that allow you to observe and chart children's progress in both academic and non-academic skills include

- multi-sensory teaching
- focused discussion
- enrichment activities
- extension activities
- circletime discussion
- questioning techniques.

Staff at an urban junior school, with 261 children on role, recognised that they had not identified any child in their school as having exceptional ability. Statutory assessments had not revealed any outstanding achievements. Neither staff nor parents had noted any specific high ability in their children.

Staff decided to introduce weekly sessions in each class of focused discussions stimulated by specific open-ended questions. The questions were designed to elicit responses from the children that would challenge their thinking and develop these skills as defined in Curriculum 2000.

A simple open-ended question such as 'What if you woke up tomorrow morning and found that there were no trees. How would you react?' elicited a wide variety of responses, from a mixed ability Year 4 class, ranging from a complex understanding of photosynthesis to a deeply personal response. 'I'd be gutted because the tree outside my bedroom was planted by my dad just before he died.'

Tape recordings were kept of these sessions, allowing staff to identify children with exceptional thinking ability. They were also used to identify areas of support needed to develop all the children's thinking skills.

Tracking development in literacy and numeracy

In order to track whole-school development in literacy and numeracy you need to decide

- what type of tests should be used
- how frequently the tests should be administered
- who will analyse and evaluate the data gathered
- what kind of response will be made after analysis and evaluation.

You need to purchase tests that are designed for use with the same children over a number of years. Using different standardised tests from one year to another will not provide accurate comparisons. Therefore, before choosing tests you need to consider whether they are designed for use over a number of years with the same children, whether they will provide the kind of information you need in your particular school and whether they are child- and teacher-friendly.

The frequency of ongoing assessments will depend very much on the type of tests you decide to use in your school. You may choose to use summative/diagnostic tests such as Edinburgh Reading tests or Mathematics 6–14. These are standardised tests that can be used with whole classes. Parallel forms allow for year-on-year comparison. These tests give an overall assessment as well as individual diagnostic profiles.

> Staff at an urban junior school, with 282 children on role, were not satisfied with the information gained from the reading tests that were used for tracking reading progress across phases (from Key Stage 1 to Key Stage 2). With a high number of children identified as SEN when they arrived at the junior school, the staff decided to use Edinburgh Reading tests. These tests provided them with overall reading assessments as well as diagnostic profiles.
>
> After trialling the use of Edinburgh 1 with Year 3 children, the staff found that they were able to target reading support and resources more effectively by evaluating the diagnostic information given by the test.

You may decide to use a specific formative assessment tool such as GOAL. This is designed to support teachers in monitoring both individual and class progress over time. The tests are matched to National Curriculum levels and the National Literacy and Numeracy programmes of study. The tests are both child- and teacher-friendly and can be used with mixed ability groups. The tests each have about 50 items covering National Curriculum Levels 1–5 and provide ongoing assessment of children's progress in both literacy and numeracy. GOAL also provides an analysis of skills showing individual areas of strength and weakness.

Analysing and evaluating data needs to be a shared responsibility, usually carried out by the senior management team in larger primary schools. In small schools, however, it will probably mean that all teachers will be involved. If data from assessments are to have any impact on improving standards of literacy and numeracy in your school, you need to have systems that will help you to disseminate clearly what is happening in terms of levels of achievement and patterns of progress in your school. Some responses that you make to this information may need to be made at whole-school level. If, for instance, levels of achievement in reading are low across a number of year groups, then you will need to look carefully at the teaching of reading in your school as a whole. Some responses may be made at group level, such as introducing teaching strategies and techniques to motivate boys to write, if the information shows that boys are underachieving in writing. Responses may also be made at individual level.

> Joshua joined a rural town primary school, with 314 children on role, during the last term of Year 5. His previous school had assessed his National Curriculum level as level 2 across all areas of the curriculum. He had very low self-esteem and poor social interaction skills. His parents were particularly anxious about his social interaction difficulties and the apparent mis-match between what he could achieve at home with what he achieved at school.
>
> Formative assessments revealed that Joshua had a good knowledge and understanding of factual and conceptual vocabulary, particularly words related to science, maths and technology. This was born out by the fact that he scored in the 99 percentile for understanding of vocabulary using BPVS (British Picture Vocabulary Scale).
>
> Because of his difficulties with the social use of language, Joshua was referred to a Combined Communication Clinic and received a diagnosis of Asperger syndrome.
>
> Staff found that when he was given opportunities to work within calm, stable, structured routines where his abilities were recognised, he began to make progress. He was also motivated by the type of learning situation that allowed him the flexibility to develop his own approach to a task within a structured environment. For instance, when he was asked to make detailed observations by sketching a friend, he systematically started at the head and had to note every detail on that part of the body before he could move on to the next part. Joshua's ability was recognised and tracked through formative assessments and his IEP. His Key Stage 2 national test results were Level 5 in maths and science and Level 4 in English.

How to use the data gathered from tracking progress

Most schools carry out regular assessment, in addition to National Curriculum tests, but one of the common criticisms made by Ofsted is that schools do not analyse the data sufficiently or use the data to make an impact on teaching and learning. When analysing data you need to be looking for patterns of achievement.

After analysing the data, all staff need to be made aware of the findings and a plan of action agreed. This should form part of the school improvement plan. Staff training needs should be identified, both individual and whole school. Good practice should be identified both within your school and within your authority and opportunities given to staff to share this good practice. Some teaching strategies and techniques shared in this way may motivate certain groups or cohorts in your school and have a direct impact on the progress made by your children. It is important to ensure that all support staff are deployed effectively in order to help develop strengths and target weaknesses in both individuals and groups of children. Budgets need to be reviewed so that resources can be allocated to support areas of weakness.

SEN coordinators and gifted and talented coordinators need to be made aware of those children who have been identified as having strengths or weaknesses in areas not previously recognised.

How you can link tracking progress to target-setting

Tracking children's progress will have very little impact on school improvement if you do not apply the information gained to individual, group, cohort and whole-school target-setting. Tracking and target-setting should form part of your school's planning cycle. Targets for improvement need to be SMART (that is, Specific, Measurable, Achievable, Realistic and Time-related). SEN coordinators are used to setting SMART targets for individual children as part of their IEPs. However, it is important to remember that the review element of an IEP relies on the evaluation of information gained from tracking individual progress in order to be able to set new targets. Both information and targets should be shared with children and parents so that there is a clear understanding of what has been achieved and what can be achieved. For the majority of children their individual targets will be curriculum-based and can be shared within the class setting.

Whole-school targets could be related to improving the teaching and learning in a particular curriculum area or they could be related to attendance and behaviour issues. Some targets could be related to specific groups of children or cohorts who may be making less progress than others and need the provision of extra resources. The target-setting process will involve you in using the information gained from tracking progress to set individual targets, group targets, curriculum targets and whole-school targets. However, target-setting can only be effective if evaluation of the information gained from tracking progress informs teacher intervention.

A village infant school of 78 children used the following format to track the progress of each cohort of children in literacy and numeracy. Dividing the cohorts into boys and girls allowed the gender differences to be noted at the same time.

One sheet of graph paper per subject/gender/cohort was divided vertically into 'levels'. The children's names were listed down the left-hand side. At the end of the reception year a red dot was marked for each child at the level attained. Each subsequent term another dot was added to show the new level.

Presuming the average child to progress one 'level' per term you can then set annual targets at class or cohort level – two levels for low achievers, three for the average and four for the high achievers.

Reading the chart they could easily spot

- the rates of progress for each child
- those who may need a diagnostic assessment carried out to show why their rate of progress is so slow, or at a standstill
- where they need to intervene to redress the slowing up of a child who made lots of progress in the early stages
- where they needed to add challenge for the highest achievers, and so on

> After evaluating the results of their school-based maths assessments, staff at a city primary school, with 426 children on role, recognised that data-handling was an area for improvement. Both individual and cohort targets were set on a half-termly basis using the information gained from formative assessments. The children were made aware of their achievements and of what they needed to do next to make progress through a system of shared criteria. This was in the form of simple statements displayed in the classroom and related to National Curriculum levels. Individual targets were limited to two in order to ensure success and the children were encouraged to support each other in achieving their targets using practical situations where possible.

Effective teacher intervention

Effective teacher intervention in direct response to assessment/tracking information provides the foundation for school improvement. It is important that strengths are recognised and celebrated in order for staff to have the confidence to improve weaknesses. Sharing good practice is an excellent way of developing effective intervention skills. This also helps staff become aware of issues relating to teaching and learning within the context of whole school philosophy, aims and objectives.

The Scottish CCC, in their consultation paper of 1996, identified a number of ways in which effective teachers operate. These include

- quality of teaching and teacher intervention
- understanding of individual teaching and learning styles
- ability to establish and maintain good quality relationships with children
- understanding of the way individual children think and learn
- talking regularly with learners about their learning, and listening to them
- developing a climate in the classroom that involves maintaining order without undermining learners' self-esteem
- effective organisation and management of children and resources
- sharing own preferred learning style with children
- knowledge about subject, topic links and educational research.

These points put as much emphasis on the quality of learning as they do on the quality of teaching and it is important to remember this when looking at intervention practices. When you plan activities aimed at enhancing progress you need to consider using a number of recognised effective strategies and techniques such as the following.

Motivation strategies – these could include setting fun challenges, individual, group and class reward systems, linking learning to real experiences, enrichment sessions and using ICT as an integral part of lessons.

Measurement criteria – your children should always be aware of the criteria used for measuring their achievements. This means that you should share the learning objectives at the start of each lesson and then revisit them during the plenary. Learning objectives can be simple 'I can' statements for younger children or children with learning difficulties. By sharing the learning objectives your children can measure their own progress over the course of time.

Mind-mapping – if a mind map is constructed at the start of a unit of work it is an effective way of showing children where they have come from and where they are going. It helps to make them aware of the 'big picture' and allows them to place their learning within a recognisable context. You need to start with a blank sheet and ask the children to tell you all that they know about the topic for study. Then ask them to suggest links that can be made between the different areas of their knowledge. As the study develops both you and the children can add in other links to their learning. If visual symbols are used then children with reading difficulties can access the information more easily.

Modes of learning – most children have a preferred learning style or a way of learning that suits them best (see Chapter 2). Some children have a dominant learning style and have difficulty accessing information unless they are able to use this style. You need to vary activities in order to accommodate the range of learning styles in your classroom. It is important that you provide opportunities for all your children to use the learning style that suits them best when learning new skills.

Multi-sensory strategies – these are teaching strategies that allow your children to use their senses in an integrated way through activities that provide a multi-sensory experience.

> Through INSET, led by the SEN coordinator at a small town primary school with 189 children on role, staff were made aware of the benefits of using a multi-sensory approach in their teaching. While studying the solar system in their science lessons, Year 5 children were given opportunities to
>
> - watch original footage of moon walks and talk about the implications of space travel
> - listen to extracts from *The Planets* suite by Holst while drawing a diagram of the solar system
> - link their own musical compositions to their knowledge of the planets
> - explore movement in time and space using their own bodies
> - produce mobiles of the solar system showing an understanding of relative distance.
>
> These activities allowed the children to use their senses in an integrated way and enhance their learning.

Tracking gifted and SEN children

Gifted children

Tracking the progress of gifted children can often be quite a challenge. Those who are academically gifted, particularly in the areas of maths, science and English, can usually be tracked through test data analysis and regular sampling of work. However, many children have talents that are not easily observable in school. They may be talented musicians, or talented in a sport not played at school. There are a number of checklists available, based on Gardner's multiple intelligences, that can be shared with both parents and children to identify talent.

Tracking talent development often requires liaison with specialists in their field and this is where support groups like NACE are helpful. A significant number of gifted children underachieve at school, either because they do not want to appear different or because they find the curriculum undemanding and boring. It is important that you provide opportunities that will challenge and inspire your children to develop their abilities to their full potential. If you provide suitable activities, you will be able to observe, record and track the development of skills in your gifted children and note how well they transfer and generalise these skills in a variety of situations. These could include

- stimulating enrichment activities
- challenging extension activities
- intriguing investigation activities
- a wide range of activities involving thinking skills.

SEN children

Tracking the progress of SEN children has tended to rely very much on identification of need through summative assessments, then individual diagnostic assessments, followed by the setting up of programmes of support work with inbuilt teacher assessments. IEP targets related to the support work and regular reviews of progress were made in the light of the information gained from teacher assessments. The introduction of P Scales has provided a way of tracking the progress of those children who are working below National Curriculum level 1. By using P Scales as regular summative assessments, individual, group and cohort profiles can be set up to monitor progress. One LEA has taken the P Scales and organised them into simple 'can do' statements.

So remember…

1. Tracking progress is about gathering information about individual children on a regular basis. This information should be used to evaluate their needs and monitor the effectiveness of the teaching and learning in your school.

2. Assessments used for tracking progress should comprise a balance of
   - summative assessment
   - formative assessment
   - diagnostic assessment.

3. You need to use teaching strategies and techniques that give you opportunities to chart your children's progress in non-academic as well as academic areas.

4. You need to choose literacy and numeracy tests that will help you to analyse levels of achievement and patterns of progress in your school.

5. Analysis of test data should always have an impact on teaching and learning in your school.

6. Target-setting can only be effective if evaluation of the information gained from tracking progress informs teacher intervention.

7. Teacher intervention, in response to assessment/tracking information, should reflect recognised effective teaching strategies and techniques in order to enhance your children's learning.

8. Profiles of learning need to be compiled for gifted and SEN children in order to monitor their progress effectively.

4 Assessment for special purposes

Assessment for special purposes can be part of whole-class assessment or it may need to be additional to general classroom monitoring and tracking. It really means looking at specific groups of children or individuals who may, for a range of reasons, cause you or others some concern, or who may indeed be identified as a result of whole-class assessment.

In this chapter, there is information on

- why you need to assess for special purposes
- who should be assessed for special purposes
- how to organise assessment for special purposes.

This chapter contains practical strategies for

- selecting appropriate assessment strategies
- planning for the needs of specific groups of children
- using assessment to remove barriers to learning.

Why you need to assess for special purposes

To inform classroom planning and differentiation

'The key to meeting the needs of all children lies in the teacher's knowledge of each child's skills and abilities and the teacher's ability to match this knowledge to finding ways of providing appropriate access to the curriculum for every child.'
(DfES, 2001, para. 5:37)

The majority of children in your class can be tracked using the school's standard assessment procedures, but it will be necessary for you to have access to some additional strategies for use with individuals or groups of children who need more detailed assessment. Such additional monitoring and diagnosis of children's specific needs, whatever they may be, will then enable you to pinpoint more carefully your planning and teaching of these children to help them progress appropriately.

> Claudia came into a year 4 class, having been educated previously in a private school abroad. She appeared to be a quiet, amenable and happy pupil. However, it soon became apparent that she was not responding as expected to all her learning opportunities and that she was therefore not fully accessing the curriculum. She had excellent spelling, reading and handwriting, but these highly developed skills did not seem to equip her for wider learning. Moreover, she seemed to need to watch her classmates and follow their lead in practical situations. Gradually, her classteacher also realised that, whilst appearing to be reading fluently, she was not able to answer any questions about her reading or give her response to it.
>
> As a result of these observations, the classteacher decided to give her a reading comprehension test (one which the whole class had completed together before her arrival). This showed straight away that her comprehension reading age was more than three years behind her chronological age. The next step was to ask a teaching assistant to observe her in the classroom situation over a whole session, noting down her responses and how she managed her work. This clearly demonstrated that Claudia was not responding to the directions of the classteacher, but rather that she followed and copied what her classmates were doing. Similarly, when undertaking a task, she placed heavy reliance on the support and lead of a friend who sat next to her. When asked a question, she shook her head and said she didn't know. When asked to read out loud, she read with expression, but did not demonstrate understanding of the content in the task which followed. When asked to put a piece of work away in her drawer, she was unable to do so, trying repeatedly to 'post' it in the wrong way around and needing her friend to do it for her.
>
> These and other detailed observation notes helped the teacher to identify that Claudia appeared to have communication and spatial difficulties. Using the evidence she had collected, the classteacher took her concerns to the SEN coordinator, who arranged for her to be assessed by the educational psychologist. This duly happened and the ensuing assessment report confirmed that she had a severe language disorder, together with spatial and fine-motor control difficulties.

The National Curriculum guidance is to be flexible in your approach. This might mean selecting content and skills from earlier or later levels or key stages, as appropriate, 'so that individual children can make progress and show what they can achieve' (DfEE, 1999, p.30).

To initiate the process of special needs assessments and interventions by the SEN coordinator and specialist support

If your assessment evidence indicates that the adaptation of the curriculum or individualisation of work needs to go beyond general differentiation, you will need to liaise with the SEN coordinator. It will be his or her responsibility to arrange for more in-depth diagnosis and support of a child's needs, possibly involving outside professionals, such as educational psychologists, who will use specialised strategies and materials.

To inform the writing of IEPs and to set targets

The assessment of the specific needs of individuals or groups of children will be very helpful when setting individual or group targets for learning. Some of these children may be identified as having special educational needs and will therefore require IEPs, which will need to specify their learning targets as agreed between you and the SEN coordinator. The parents and children will also have a strong input to target-setting and will equally be supported by clear assessment evidence and linked recommendations.

Who should be assessed for special purposes?

When inspectors report on the school's progress, they will be required to highlight the achievement of different groups of children. In order to do this they will look particularly at

> 'The achievement of children of different capabilities, especially those with special educational needs (and) the relative achievement of boys and girls, and different groups and individuals, especially those from different ethnic backgrounds, and those whose home language is not English.'
> (Ofsted, 2003, p36)

In addition to these special groups of children, you will probably develop concerns about individual children in your class from time to time. Sometimes, your concerns will have a known cause and you will want to assess how the child's learning and progress are being affected by such factors.

On other occasions, you may become aware that a child appears to be slowing or halting their rate of progress, or even regressing, without knowing of any reason for this. You need to know how the child is doing now compared both to prior attainment and to previous rates of progress.

You may well develop concerns over how one of your more able children is doing, in comparison to their potential. Occasionally, even a gifted child will 'coast' or underachieve, for a variety of reasons, to the extent that you may not initially be aware of their high ability.

> The range of standard classroom assessments showed that Joseph, a child in Year 3, was making steady progress across the curriculum. However, his new classteacher developed the suspicion that he was finding everything quite easy and that he was not needing to put any effort into his work. She noticed also that Joseph was increasingly inclined to play the class clown. This didn't seem to have any effect on the quality of his work, but did seriously distract others in the class.
>
> The teacher suspected that Joseph might be more able that he was showing, especially in maths, and decided to set him a series of maths challenges to assess his thinking and problem-solving skills, as well as his understanding of higher-level concepts. Joseph took on these tasks with obvious enjoyment and showed that he was able to meet the challenges he had been set. His attitude was positive and he seemed to be more engrossed in his work than usual.
>
> Next, the teacher set him (and the rest of the class) a cognitive ability test, in which he achieved a standardised score of 137, which was well above the average of 100, around which most of his classmates' scores clustered. The teacher took this evidence to discuss with the school's gifted and talented coordinator, who put Joseph on the gifted and talented register and provided some materials which the class teacher could use with him. He was invited to join the maths extension group, which met once a week to undertake special investigations.

Usually, the need to assess specific individuals or groups of children will be initiated by your own concerns. However, there may be occasions when parents or other members of staff may nominate an individual child who they believe to be experiencing difficulties you were not fully aware of (with homework, for example), or who demonstrates high ability outside school, but prefers not to show this in the classroom.

Children you might want to assess for special purposes

- Children you suspect may have SEN.
- SEN children whose progress needs to be closely monitored in line with their IEPs.
- Children about whom you or colleagues develop new or temporary concerns.
- Children who have failed to make the progress expected of them.
- Children who you suspect may be 'coasting' or underachieving.
- Children who you feel may have gifts or talents.
- Children whose parents have requested or suggested detailed assessment.
- Children with emotional and/or behavioural difficulties.
- Children who have English as an additional or second language.
- Children from different ethnic groups.
- Children with physical difficulties or disabilities.
- Children of high mobility, such as Traveller children.

How to organise assessment for special purposes

Using additional expertise

You will want to enlist the help of the SEN coordinator or other colleagues to assess in more depth or in special situations. If you are lucky enough to have the support of a teaching assistant, there are a number of ways you can involve her in individual or small-group assessment. You may be able to make use of volunteer helpers or the child's own parents to take part in some of the assessment activities.

Some of the outside professionals may be willing to be consulted at an early stage to help with classroom observations and other informal strategies, in order to agree what further assessment and diagnosis may be needed.

> Gamal came into the Reception class with a bang! He clearly had ability and made good progress with his stepping stones, but from the outset he had difficulty making friends or relating to other children, and was inclined to temper-tantrums and wild outbursts of aggressive behaviour. Gamal's father worked away from home. His mother did not appear to feel she should tell him what to do or what not to do and he seemed bewildered by the idea of rules at school. Many of the other children in his class were quite frightened of him and especially the unpredictable nature of his moods. For Gamal, English was an additional language, his main language at home being Arabic.
>
> Gamal's classteacher felt that he lacked social skills, had low self-esteem, despite seeming quite sure of himself, and had a negative attitude to any group activities. She observed Gamal's behaviour and responses in the classroom and enlisted a student on work experience to observe him informally in the playground. After some fruitful discussions, they were able to form a fuller picture of Gamal's difficulties, the main points of which the teacher described, with lots of examples of observed behaviours, in a written report. This provided evidence that she could then discuss with others in the school.
>
> Gamal's teacher initially asked his mother to come and discuss the situation, but this was difficult because her command of English was poor and she seemed completely unaware that his attitude might cause him or his classmates any problems.
>
> The teacher went to discuss her concerns and difficulties with the headteacher, who immediately sought the help of the LEA's support services and obtained the input of both a Behavioural Support advisory teacher to observe Gamal at school and an Arabic-speaking Education Welfare Officer to talk about the situation with his mother at home. Both of these professionals fed back their findings to the class teacher and the SEN coordinator. This created a much more positive atmosphere and a clearer understanding of the problems all round. With some practical advice from the Behavioural Support advisory teacher, the classteacher was now able to plan a series of sessions with a teaching assistant to develop Gamal's social skills and to help him make friends in the Reception class.

Your assessments will provide you with evidence to share with professionals or with the child's parents as you identify more precisely what his needs are and how to meet them.

Whole-class or individual assessments?

Although many assessments for special purposes will inevitably need to be individual or in small groups, some types of assessment can be done in whole-class situations and this is obviously advisable wherever possible, for practical reasons. Additionally, such assessments can quite often be more useful than expected if the whole class takes part, as one or more other children may also be revealed as having similar difficulties or abilities.

Adopting an objective approach

There are a number of factors which will help you to avoid making judgements based on preconceptions or misinterpretations. There are also steps you can take to enable fairer comparisons to be drawn and to clarify findings.

When assessing

- use annual or other regular tests in the same conditions as far as possible every time, so that the results can be more closely comparable

- always use the individual's prior attainment as a starting point (rather than age-related averages) to gauge individual performance

- be honest and rigorous in analysing and interpreting the outcomes of assessment, even (or especially) if they don't show the results you expected or hoped for

- be open to the unexpected

- use qualitative data carefully as it may be a subjective or poorly informed judgement, especially if it involves observations or opinions from non-professionals

- use colour-coding to highlight key findings (eg. when analysing data in a chart, use green print or highlighter for high progress; red for low progress, which suggests the need for immediate intervention)

- always look at the whole picture, so as to have a framework for interpretation

- keep all test-papers and raw scores until outcomes have been verified (in case of inadvertent miscalculations or misinterpretations) and to enable more detailed analysis if this is found to be necessary.

Selecting appropriate assessment strategies

Some forms of assessment will be used throughout the school on a regular basis. As well as being useful to analyse whole year-group progress and attainment, they will form part of the process of tracking individual progress. In some cases, they may also provide the first indications that there may be a slowing of progress and that there might be underlying problems that need further, more detailed assessment and investigation.

Foundation Stage Profiles give an ideal opportunity to pick up any potential difficulties there might be in any of the six areas of learning. The stepping stones provide a clear path of progression at these early stages and are a useful framework by which to judge early progress.

End of key stage tasks and tests are the next nation-wide forms of assessment. These tests are standardised and therefore give an opportunity to compare a cohort, group or individual's performance against all and similar groups across the region or the country as a whole. Many LEAs also provide breakdowns of the skills covered by each question or task and this can be very helpful when analysing the strengths and weaknesses in an individual child's performance. Similarly, optional assessment tasks across Key Stage 2 can be used in this way, to track performance in English and maths through the key stage.

Other forms of assessment can also be obtained in the core subjects and your school may well have set up assessments as part of its schemes of work across the whole curriculum. These assessments can also help to highlight a particular child's strengths and weaknesses, as well as the progress of groups of children, such as those of multi-ethnic origin or those for whom English is an additional language.

Indeed, English as an additional language (EAL) may in itself be a significant barrier to assessment, which is where the non-verbal elements of cognitive ability or reasoning tests can be particularly useful in identifying the ability and potential of children with little fluency in English.

A variety of standardised tests in reading and spelling are widely available, many of which can be used for whole-class assessment. These whole-class tests are a useful and practical starting point and in analysing the outcomes of these standardised tests you can identify those individuals or groups you may wish to focus on for more detailed assessment.

Cognitive ability, or reasoning tests, in their many forms, can be very useful in highlighting the areas of difficulty a particular child may be experiencing, as well as his areas of strength. At Key Stage 1, you could use a battery of tests in different skill areas with individuals or groups, using the computer or practical classroom situations to show each child's strengths and weaknesses.

A whole year group's reading test scores were collated and analysed in a number of ways. The table of results showed

- each individual child's reading age in this test
- his reading age exactly one year ago (in similar circumstances on the same test)
- his chronological age now
- the difference between his chronological age and his reading age in this test
- the progress in years and/or months between last year's and this year's reading tests
- the whole year-group's averages for all of the above classifications
- break-downs of all of the above for specific groups – SEN children, boys/girls, EAL children, any children who had been given daily sessions with a mentor and any other relevant groups.

Using this data, the assessment coordinator and the classteacher together were able to highlight in red and select those children who were most in need of intensive support. Reading mentors were recruited who were volunteers willing to give up half an hour or more per day to work with the same children each day on their reading. This system worked so well that others wanted to join it too! One Year 2 boy asked his teacher 'Can I have a lady of my own?' The children who had been given their own reading mentors for daily practice were shown, in the next year's standardised reading test, to have made significantly improved progress, both compared to their previous year's performance and compared to those who had not been part of this scheme. With this evidence, the reading mentor approach was extended across the whole school, with parents keen to volunteer when they could see how much improvement children made on it.

Lucid CoPS allows you to select just those areas about which you may have concerns related to a particular child. The selected tests can be done in the form of child-friendly computer games with a teaching assistant to show a detailed profile of the child's performance in these areas for further analysis. (Lucid also produce a similar battery of tests for Key Stage 2 called *LASS Junior*.)

At Key Stage 2, cognitive ability or reasoning tests can be administered in blanket fashion across a whole class to show the range of ability and potential you have in the class as well as individuals' performance. This type of test will often highlight those children who have particularly high ability but are either unable or unwilling to show their ability in their school work. It will also be especially helpful in identifying discrepancies between children's verbal and non-verbal abilities, which can often be the first step in identifying children who are not achieving their potential and who may, for example, have a specific learning difficulty or perhaps a language disorder.

Another very useful reasoning test for use in Key Stages 1 and 2 is *CAT 3*, produced by nferNelson, which includes verbal, non-verbal and quantitative tests. These are very easy to score and the publishers also provide a computerised analysis service which returns a comprehensive set of test results and a guide to children's cognitive abilities.

For children with special educational needs who are performing below Level 1 of the National Curriculum, the SEN coordinator will probably introduce you to the P scales, which are now available across the curriculum (DfEE/QCA, 2001). These P scales break down stages of achievement into small steps in graduated levels.

Within subject areas, there are a number of useful strategies for analysing the details of children's difficulties. One such example is Miscue Analysis in reading, which is a way of identifying which reading cues a child uses predominantly and which they have most weakness in. You could administer this yourself, but it is quite time-consuming and it might be better if you or the SEN coordinator can train a particular teaching assistant to specialise in this throughout the school. You will find the ensuing analysis very useful in highlighting areas to target.

Whenever possible, the class teacher will want to take note of the children's own perceptions of themselves and their learning experiences. These self-assessments will tell you a lot about children's attitudes towards their learning and their own perceived strengths and weaknesses. They should also help you to identify each child's preferred learning styles.

Last, but certainly not least, teacher assessment and classroom or small group observations (including audio-taped discussions and videos of children at

---

The table below shows the scores of children in a Year 3 class who completed Hodder and Stoughton's user-friendly *Reasoning Progress Tests* (names have been changed, but scores are genuine examples).

In this table, Ben is shown to have a significantly higher non-verbal than verbal score, which indicates the possibility of some kind of problem. In fact, the class teacher was alarmed by such a wide difference between the two scores of a child she had previously thought was achieving the most of a limited potential, but now realised that he had a much greater non-verbal ability than she had formerly suspected. She decided to investigate this discrepancy further, initially by asking a teaching assistant to undertake some further non-verbal tasks with him and to observe his responses.

The teacher shared these two forms of evidence in a discussion with the SEN coordinator, who agreed that further investigation should be carried out at a more specialised level, which was immediately put into effect. The outcome was that Ben was diagnosed as having quite a severe specific learning difficulty (dyslexia), for which he was given intensive specialist support. Meanwhile, his teacher was able to plan his learning more effectively by building on his non-verbal strengths across the curriculum.

Year 3 Reasoning Tests

	Non-verbal reasoning	Verbal reasoning
Ben Matlock	120	93
Andrew Clay	117	100
Georgina Andrews	111	117
Tim Prowse	98	118
Ajay Foster	93	71
Rosie Wallis	87	101
Sam Miller	81	86

work) are some of the most crucial elements in assessing the performance and progress of children at every stage. Whether a child has physical, behavioural, emotional or learning difficulties, focused observation can provide you with some of your most valuable and relevant assessment evidence about individual children.

All of this information can be very helpful in completing the picture of the performance and progress of an individual or group of children, as well as providing a clearer focus for the next steps in planning their future learning.

Planning for the needs of specific groups of children

All kinds of assessment may form part of the profiles of individuals and groups of children and all will help towards the identification and analysis of children's strengths and weaknesses.

Assessment as a diagnostic tool

Various forms of assessment can highlight aspects of a child's needs and together they will paint a picture that shows the SEN coordinator and other professionals which directions to take to diagnose that child's learning difficulties. These difficulties may take many forms and are collectively known as 'barriers to learning'. If you think a child in your class may need more specialist assessment, share your assessment evidence with the SEN coordinator and discuss the next steps.

Target-setting for children with SEN

For the children who have special educational needs, their targets can be specified in their IEPs and form the focus for more specific support. For these SEN children, you will be required to undertake regular reviews with the SEN coordinator and others, probably including the child's parents. Any children you may have with statements of special educational needs will be the subject of more formal annual reviews as well. In every case, the targets set will be crucial in measuring progress and achievement and will also help raise self-esteem. Setting appropriate targets and evaluating the child's progress are therefore very important and you can only do that if you have the fullest possible up-to-date knowledge about the child's performance and progress, as a result of the assessment work you have done.

Tracking progress

Tracking children's ongoing progress is discussed in detail in Chapter 3. Tracking is particularly important for those individuals and groups of children for whom there are special reasons to keep a closer eye on their performance.

> Dan was a Year 5 child who had always been reluctant to read and his reading age was now about eighteen months behind his chronological age. Worse, Dan seemed to have stalled with his reading, despite daily practice with a reading mentor and strong support from his parents. His self-esteem was low and his reading difficulties were now beginning increasingly to affect his learning across the curriculum. However, he had been assessed by the LEA literacy support service, who reported that, although he is eighteen months behind, this was not sufficient to trigger their involvement.
>
> Dan's classteacher, who had recently done a course on reading development, decided to try a miscue analysis with him. This showed that Dan had clear strengths in using his phonic and graphic skills when reading, but at this higher readability level, his comprehension had decreased and the miscue analysis showed that he had a weakness in using his semantic skills to predict unknown words from the context and meaning of the surrounding text.
>
> Using this assessment evidence, together with some of the materials she had learned about on her course, the classteacher planned a programme of semantic activities for Dan, including some games, which his parents agreed to help him with at home. Over the next few months, Dan worked hard at this new programme of work and gradually seemed to derive greater understanding and enjoy his reading more, which did a great deal for his self-esteem as well. By the end of Year 6, Dan's reading age was only four months below his chronological age and he was able to access the full range of curriculum learning opportunities.

Planning learning opportunities

Classroom assessment will be the main guide for planning the learning opportunities for your class. This will involve appropriate levels of differentiation and your own assessments of the children's attainment will enable you to focus the learning for each group within your class. Where necessary, you may be required to vary the levels further to practise skills and consolidate learning or to extend and challenge your more able children. For the vast majority of your children, year by year, this will be manageable, but occasionally you will have a more daunting situation that requires more than mere differentiation. If this is the case, you should seek, at the earliest opportunity, the help of either the SEN coordinator or the gifted and talented coordinator in your school. They will be able to suggest more individualised programmes of work to be done with a teaching assistant or provide more appropriate learning materials.

Using assessment to remove barriers to learning

When planning

If you are in a school with more than one class for each age group, you will be able to discuss assessment with your year-team colleagues. Such liaison can be very helpful, both in agreeing what assessments to undertake, planning when and how to do them and analysing the outcomes. Pool your ideas about which individuals and groups you should assess in more detail and what to do with your assessment outcomes to make your task much easier and more pleasant. One of the key features will be to plan at what points in your curriculum schemes of work you should add in assessments that will give you the information you require.

Liaising with others

Within the school, you will find it helpful to liaise with the SEN coordinator, the gifted and talented coordinator, the assessment coordinator, mentors or teaching assistants on a regular basis, both in the assessment of and the planning for children with special educational needs or gifts and talents. In this way, you will be able to help those children to overcome the barriers to their learning.

Beyond the school, liaise with other professionals who are involved with any child, such as educational psychologists, specialist teachers, health professionals and so on.

What you do with your assessment outcomes regarding specific individuals or groups of children could make a lot of difference when it comes to the experiences you can provide for them over the weeks and months to follow. By coordinating your efforts with your colleagues and ensuring continuity, you will also provide the optimum platform for their future educational development through the school.

Recognising success

Assessment should lead to the recognition and celebration of progress, especially for those children who have become more used to making little or no progress in some aspects of their work.

The QCA guidance (2001) suggests that progress may be recognised when children with learning difficulties

- develop increasingly effective ways to communicate from the concrete towards the abstract

- develop a range of increasingly effective responses to social interactions, from resistance, through passive cooperation to active participation

---

Holly came into the Reception class without any pre-school or nursery experience. Her Reception teacher, therefore, had not previously known that she did not speak. The usual term for this is either elective or selective mutism. She seemed happy enough to be at school and to be on the sidelines of every activity, but steadfastly refused to say anything to anybody. When other children approached her to join in their games, she did so, shyly. When asked a question she either nodded, shook her head or adopted a glazed expression, but she never smiled. Indeed, she rarely even looked at the teacher or nursery nurse. When directed towards a task, she acquiesced. When praised for something she had done, such as putting a puzzle away, she just stood and looked down at the floor as usual.

Holly's teacher decided to ask her nursery nurse to spend some time every day with Holly, playing games and looking at stories together, one to one. The nursery nurse did not push Holly to respond, but encouraged her as much as possible in a low-key, natural way. The nursery nurse reported daily back to the teacher and kept a record of Holly's responses to their activities. The nursery nurse felt that Holly enjoyed these special times, but there was no evidence beyond intuition. Still Holly did not smile.

One day, after about three weeks of their daily half-hour sessions together, the nursery nurse praised Holly for completing an activity and Holly looked up at her, maintaining eye-contact for a minute or more. This was a breakthrough! The nursery nurse noted what she had said and how Holly had responded in her daily record. The next day she planned a similar situation and was rewarded with the same response. Over the next few days, the nursery nurse built in as many such situations as she could, based on her initial observation, and Holly rewarded her with increased periods of eye contact. Finally, the day came when Holly smiled. The nursery nurse gave her quiet but warm praise. The teacher did the same. Before long Holly was smiling in the classroom during lesson times. She smiled more and more. Soon she began to whisper. The careful observations of Holly's early responses forged the way for her to make very small steps of progress, which could be recognised and celebrated and which became bigger steps as time went on.

- develop a range of responses to actions, events or experiences, even when there appears to be little progress in acquiring knowledge and skills
- demonstrate and repeat a new achievement in varied circumstances
- demonstrate an increase in knowledge and understanding about a subject
- demonstrate the ability to maintain, refine, generalise or combine skills
- move from a dependence on secure routines toward a greater degree of autonomy, shown by risk-taking and increased confidence
- demonstrate a reduced need for support
- show a reduction in the frequency or severity of behaviour difficulties
- make the active decision not to participate or respond (in the case of a child who was previously passive).

Praise and rewards systems

Praise and rewards systems should form a key part of your planning. This will be most effective if it is based on pinpointing what progress children have been making, where they are now, what their agreed individual or group targets are and your expectations of them (and their expectations of themselves). Use them appropriately, not so often that they become commonplace and thus lose their value in the child's mind, but often enough to encourage them to continue to make the best progress possible.

So remember...

1. After analysing whole-class assessment outcomes, use the data and other observations to identify individuals or particular groups of children for further or more specific assessment.

2. Select relevant assessment strategies.

3. Enlist the help of a teaching assistant and/or parents if appropriate.

4. Record findings and analyse outcomes.

5. Share these with parents, and the child if appropriate.

6. Use assessment findings as starting points for lesson planning and differentiation.

7. Consult the SEN coordinator or gifted and talented coordinator about any individual who causes you particular concern.

8. Set targets and review them regularly.

9. Praise and reward for even small steps of progress.

5 Using summative assessment

Summative assessment gives a snapshot picture of where each child is at any particular point in their education. Currently in primary schools we gather statutory summative assessment data at the end of each stage – the Foundation Stage Profile (FSP) as the children leave the Foundation or Reception class, and the Standard Assessment Tests and tasks (SATs or national tests) in Years 2 and 6.

In this chapter there is information on

- why we need to collect summative data
- how to use the summative data that you receive
- collecting summative data.

This chapter contains practical strategies for

- using the data at a whole-school level
- keeping parents informed.

Why we need to collect summative data

Most assessment in primary classrooms is formative but statutory assessment was introduced following the introduction of the National Curriculum in 1988. This caused much debate in education and led to a wide variety of views about what was to be done with the information gained from such assessment. The publishing of 'league tables' caused, and still causes, widespread concern in the education world. Finding ways of making public information on tests and examinations fair and reliable is a challenge. Comparing schools simply on the basis of test or examination results is now widely accepted as unfair. Schools serving more socially and economically advantaged areas clearly have a head start. Equally, there is evidence to suggest that certain groups of children are disadvantaged within the school curriculum. Research evidence suggests, for example, that girls are often disadvantaged by the design of tests and examinations. Also children with certain special educational needs don't always receive the support they should. Ethnicity is also an issue in which inequalities have been extensively researched.

One way to overcome these differences is by looking at the 'value added' that the school has achieved – that is, looking at the rate of progress made by individual children after they have entered school. This gives an indication of the value a school has added to the education and achievements of its children over a period of time. This is a complex area, one that is likely to take time to develop, but one that will show the true value a school can add to the education of its children. To do this, school leaders need information, and this information comes from summative tests. In any school these can include

- Foundation Stage Profile
- End of Key Stage 1 statutory assessment
- Year 3 QCA optional tests
- Year 4 QCA optional tests
- Year 5 QCA optional tests
- End of Key Stage 2 statutory assessment.

There may also be individual standardised reading and spelling tests as appropriate.

How to use the summative data that you receive

One of the most effective ways of receiving this information is to meet with the teacher who gathered it together. So, if you are a teacher in Year 1 you need to meet with the teacher from the Reception class, and so on. This is more difficult to arrange if the children are transferring from another school, or from a number of pre-school providers, but is worth any effort involved.

The teacher can talk through the children's results. They can highlight any concerns, any data that could be misleading – the child who was absent from school for the month before the Key Stage 1 national tests, the child who produced an unusually good piece of creative writing on the day, the child who is nervous and worried himself almost sick on the day of the Key Stage 2 national test maths paper.

Your school may have a system for recording summative data on tables or charts that track a child's progress. (See Chapter 3 of this handbook for practical details about doing this.) Look through these tables and note any patterns. The rate of progress can be just as useful as the actual attainment. This information will help you to do the following.

- To set the children for maths and English at least. It will help you to decide on the children who will support and yet challenge each other.
- To set targets for the children. The information about the rate of progress will help you as you pitch the level of challenge for each child.
- To plan your lessons. Some children may need to revisit earlier work, others will be advancing at great speed and will need a broader approach to stimulate and challenge their thinking and their skills. You will have outline medium-term plans which you can now fine-tune to match these particular children.

Collecting summative data

If you are a Reception class teacher you will need to complete the Foundation Stage Profile. Although you will be amassing the data for this from your own observations of the child over the year, and from information from the child's pre-school provider, it will give a picture of the child's position at the end of the Foundation Stage. This will inform the Year 1 teacher about the child's levels of attainment as they enter Key Stage 1. Your school may also carry out a baseline assessment on entry into the Reception class. This information is for internal school use only and will not need to be reported as it is no longer a statutory requirement.

If you are teaching Year 2 or Year 6 you will be carrying out the tests and tasks connected with the national tests. At the start of the school year (usually around October) you should receive your copy of the QCA handbook *Assessment and Reporting Arrangements* for that particular year. Read this carefully. It will give you information about when to carry out the tests and what they will entail. You can plan your teaching around this to make sure that you have covered all of the work necessary. It will tell you about any arrangements you should make for children who have special educational needs or who are gifted and talented. Your LEA should offer training to update you on any changes. Be sure to attend this.

If you are teaching Years 3, 4 or 5 you may be required to administer the QCA optional tests. This is a school-based decision. It does provide you with useful stepping stones to chart the child's progress between the ends of the two key stages. It is easy for a child to start falling behind and if this continues over three years the results at the end of Key Stage 2 can be disappointing for the child and their parents, and for your school's results.

Any teacher may be required to carry out other norm-referenced testing. There will be a whole-school policy about this. These tests must be carried out within the strict guidelines set down by the publisher if they are to give valid results. Make sure that you use them as and when designated by the publisher/compiler, and that you follow the instructions closely. They are most frequently used to give information about reading and spelling ability.

Using the data at a whole-school level

Statutory summative assessment was introduced as part of the National Curriculum process and we are currently measuring attainment at the age of five, in all aspects of their learning, and at seven and eleven in the core subjects of English, mathematics and science. These provide information on overall achievement in these subjects at the end of each key stage and we then make judgements about the progress that has been made.

This has caused controversy. Teachers complain that the tests are too time-consuming and disrupt the curriculum. Both teachers and parents are worried about the fairness of the tests and the reporting of such tests in league-table format that provides a rank order of schools based on their results.

However, while recognising that by far the most important method of assessment is that of a formative or diagnostic type, there is a place for summative testing in schools. Schools are starting to use these standardised assessments as part of the school self-evaluation process, as recognised by the Chief Inspector of Schools in his annual report of February 2002.

> 'Procedures for monitoring and supporting pupils' academic progress are satisfactory in about four in five schools having full inspections. The results from national tests and optional tests provide schools with the information they need to calculate the progress made by pupils year by year. It is now possible to set realistic, yet challenging targets for individuals, groups of pupils, year cohorts and the school as a whole. Some head teachers have developed effective target-setting or other systems for monitoring progress but these are strengths in less than half of the schools ... The quality and use of assessment remain the weakest aspect of teaching. Many schools are generating a great deal of assessment data, at considerable cost in terms of time, but are not using it to set work based on the pupils' prior attainment or set appropriate targets for different groups of pupils.'

John Abbot (1999), however, has a different view. He questions the whole process of knowledge-based learning and assessment.

> 'The test of successful education is not the amount of knowledge that a pupil takes away from school but his appetite to know and his capacity to learn. If the school sends out children with the desire for knowledge and some idea about how to acquire and use it, it will have done its work. Too many leave school with the appetite killed and the mind loaded with undigested lumps of information.'

So what can we do to ensure that we use summative assessment data effectively without it becoming all-powerful, taking over and leading us to lose sight of what we know is important in education?

The following case study follows the approach to this problem by the headteacher of a successful rural primary school.

When I took up my post, the school was ensuring that nearly every child at the end of Key Stage 2 was reaching the national average of Level 4 in the core subjects, placing us at the top of the league tables – a very favourable position to be in, you may think. Looking at prior attainment, however, it soon became clear that the school should be achieving at a much higher level than it was, so although the league tables showed us to be a very good school, we were, in fact, underachieving! Teacher expectation of children was low and no use was made of the assessment data we had.

The first thing I looked at was the assessment and monitoring processes in school. The staff and I looked at the standardised testing we used and the purpose we used it for. It soon became clear that the assessment data we gathered was useful in that it gave us an indication of the relative position of each pupil nationally. However, no further use was made of the data other than to identify children who may need additional intervention. As teacher expectation was low, only limited challenge was given to the children. The tests in use were not designed to give us the information we needed. Further discussion and investigation led us to the conclusion that we needed to change our method of statutory assessment so that it became relevant to the needs of the children. We decided to switch from the testing we had been using to the optional QCA test material that was becoming available. Our assessment programme was completely changed to allow us to make good use of the assessment information and track individual pupil progress, allowing us to plan more effectively.

By adopting this assessment model we began to have opportunities to track pupil progress and correlate the information we had obtained. I then had to decide how to use the data obtained so that it was relevant and useful to the teachers. Having looked at various commercially produced packages, I decided that they didn't provide the information in a way that we could usefully use so I devised an Excel spreadsheet that would. The spreadsheet contained the following data.

Level results

This allowed me to enter level results for the core subjects for each child. As the data were to be shared with the governing body's Curriculum and Assessment Committee, as part of their monitoring role, I used individual pupil numbers instead of names to identify children. We are able to enter results from the end of Key Stage 1, optional national tests results and the end of key stage results to obtain a picture of each child's attainment at each stage of learning.

UPN	Year 2		Year 3		Year 4		Year 5		Year 6	
	Maths	English	Maths	English	Maths	English	Maths	English	Maths	English
00345763	2a	2a	2a	3a	3	4	4	4	5	5

Average points scores

Here, the level results were translated into an average points score, again for each child, allowing us to check on progress as well as attainment. This gave me the opportunity to monitor attainment and progress on an individual basis, allowing opportunities to re-design the curriculum for individual children and small groups. This information also proved valuable to the school's SEN coordinator who was able to use it effectively when planning for special needs provision.

UPN	Year 2		Year 3		Year 4		Year 5		Year 6	
	Maths	English	Maths	English	Maths	English	Maths	English	Maths	English
00345763	12	12	12	18	21	27	27	27	33	33

The Assessment Handbook

Value-added information

This shows value-added information graphically to ensure progress is mapped and achievements celebrated. It also allows teachers to pinpoint any dip in performance and start asking questions to discover possible reasons why this may be happening.

This allows me to look at the position of children against national average points scores.

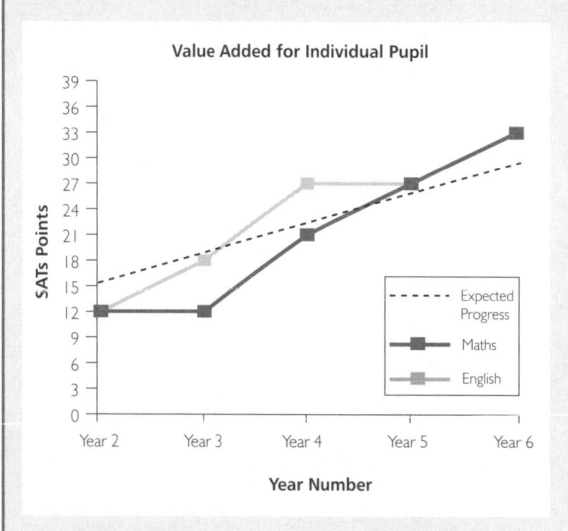

Value Added for Individual Pupil

(Graph showing SATs Points on y-axis from 0 to 39, Year Number on x-axis from Year 2 to Year 6. Lines show Expected Progress, Maths, and English.)

This graph combines all the information we keep on individual children as well as year cohorts. It enables us to track progress against the norm and allows us to make interventions where necessary. The information has proved to be a valuable tool when children move classes, although it is by no means the only one.

We still, however, have some way to go in modifying and refining this model. For example, we have already discovered that the English and maths test scores need to be broken down into component parts, ie. spelling, writing, reading, etc., so we can monitor children's progress in each of these parts more effectively.

The effects of this method of recording assessment have been very encouraging. It has provided us with data that we can use in an effective way to aid future learning, while giving us a clear indication of prior attainment. Teacher expectations have risen, teaching and learning can be referenced more easily and our planning has improved considerably, becoming much more focused. As a result, the children's attainment at the end of Key Stage 2 still reaches national averages but now, on average, over half of our children have gone on to achieve above average results at the end of Key Stage 2.

The benefits for our school

There are now clear assessment processes in place and all teachers use their knowledge of a child to identify what needs to be done in order to attain the next level. This is then fed into the medium- and short-term plans and impacts on learning. This then feeds into teachers' records, which are now far more meaningful.

When new children arrive, the information that comes with them is always used to help settle them with the minimum of disruption to their learning.

In addition to whole-cohort information, the performance of specific groups of children is monitored. For example, we found that our attainment in science was not as good as that in English and maths. Having investigated the reasons why, this is an area targeted for school development and is a key feature of the school's development and improvement plan.

The achievement of children with SEN is also tracked carefully to ensure that their progress and provision are appropriate. Children's work is scrutinised and their responses to optional tests are mapped to ensure quality of provision is maintained and improved where possible.

Benchmarking information, collated through national results, has also proved very useful in allowing us to evaluate our performance. It allows us to find similar schools who may be performing better than us in particular curriculum areas. We can then possibly visit them and share good practice – a good use of 'league tables'.

We analyse items from our Key Stage 1 tests to inform future planning, which is then used as a starting point within Key Stage 2. Even the Key Stage 2 tests are analysed to allow us to identify gaps in the teaching programme. From this process we are able to make decisions about our strategic priorities and key objectives contained in the school's development and improvement plan.

Reaching our realistic but challenging targets depends on focused attention on raising the attainment of all our children in a way that is helped considerably by the way we use our assessment data effectively. The improvements are due to the hard work of the teachers and their clarity in what assessment for learning really means, but the overview, provided by assessment data, really helps to keep us focused on what is important.

Schools wishing to use assessment data to enhance the curriculum they provide need to have a clear and coherent plan for improvement. They need to conduct a self-audit to determine strengths and areas for development.

Keeping parents informed

In good schools parents are given information about a wide variety of curriculum plans and activities. They are shown, too, how their help and encouragement can ensure that children progress with confidence and security. They will also receive information about the results of summative tests at the end of each key stage, and possibly in other year groups if you carry out the QCA optional tests or any norm-referenced tests.

Parent consultation evenings

You could use a formal parent consultation evening to share with the parents the chart that shows their child's progress – the one you use for tracking development. Show them the chart, talk about how their child is doing, their rate of progress and any concerns you may have. They may be able to explain why the child slowed down at some point when there were some problems at home. They can respond to your concerns by offering more help and encouragement at home, or supporting the school in any action you feel is necessary to address the problems.

End-of-year reports

There should be no surprises here if the parents have attended termly meetings with you and been contacted by you when you had any concerns, or pleasure, to share with them about their child's progress.

At the end of Key Stages 1 and 2 the parents will also receive the statutory forms showing the results for the whole cohort. This should have an accompanying letter to explain to them what it means, how it should be read and an interpretation of the results for your school.

Annual meeting with the governors

This is an opportunity for the parents to question you about the results for the year group. It is not an opportunity for them to talk about any one child. They can find out about the strengths and weaknesses of the school and how these will be addressed in the following year. It is a useful time to help them to understand about the way that the statistics are used. This is also a good opportunity to talk to them about the way that statistics can deflect your attention away from what really matters. They can hear about the fact that one year group differs widely from another in their strengths and that this too can affect the statistics.

For more information on sharing information with parents, see Chapter 10 of this handbook.

In conclusion

As we have seen, the use of assessment data has to be managed sensibly in order for it to become useful. Schools need to have a coherent, well-planned approach to using the ever-increasing amounts of data it accrues, otherwise it will face difficulties in trying to manage it all. All school planning should have the goal of raising child achievement at its heart and each school needs to use data to improve its quality of provision.

So remember…

- Be realistic about what you do with the ever-increasing amounts of data available.

- Have a coherent and well thought-out plan in place for developing tracking and assessment processes.

- Use comparative data constructively – make use of other schools' good practice.

- Make any system for analysing assessment data simple to understand and relevant to your particular school.

- Use assessment data to analyse trends, and track the progress of all children.

- Use assessment data to inform future planning.

6 Marking for ongoing assessment

Marking refers to the annotation and comments used when checking children's work. It provides children with information about how well they have done and where they could make improvements. It reminds you of the progress the children have made over the year. It informs parents about the rate of progress their children have made and how much support and advice they have needed to achieve their current level. As such, it is an important feature of the whole assessment cycle.

In this chapter there is information on

- why we mark children's work
- how the children respond to your marking
- how improving the marking can be of benefit.

This chapter contains practical strategies for

- making your marking more effective.

Why we mark children's work

The marking of children's work is a tool that helps them to learn and a necessary guide to you as to how well the children in your class have achieved the learning outcomes for a particular lesson or block of work.

Marking provides the child with practical information as they build a picture of their strengths and weaknesses. It can help them to recognise what they do well and where they need to improve.

Marking that is fair and informative can motivate children to want to produce high-quality work. They can recognise their own achievements and see the steps they are taking as they strive to meet challenging but achievable targets.

At the start of the lesson you will have told them what they are to learn – 'Today we will be thinking about words and phrases we can use in our writing to set the scene and how you can use them effectively.' Together you will have read examples from published writers, created some examples of your own, made lists of useful expressions and so on. You will then set the children a written task – 'You are to write the opening paragraph of a story set on a dark winter's night. It will be a description of the scene in which the story will then take place.' At this point you need to do two things. First, remind them of the learning objective as at the start of the lesson. Second, explain to them how you will be marking their work – 'As you write this opening paragraph try to include some of the words or phrases that we have talked about, or some new ones of your own. I will be looking to see how many you have included. Try to use them in such a way that I could draw a picture of the scene if I wanted to and it would look just like the picture in your mind.'

When you mark the work, mark only the way that the child has used words and phrases to set the scene. Ignore spelling, punctuation and grammar at this stage. Target the key learning points – 'You have used some interesting new phrases. I particularly like the way that you have described the clouds moving across the moon. Do you think you could improve the phrase "the trees were leaning over because of the gale"?'

How the children respond to your marking

If your marking is to have any real value it has to be meaningful to the child as well as to you and any other professional who reads your marking. Chapter 9 of this handbook explores the importance of involving the children in their own assessment in greater detail, but self-assessment begins here. Your marking is the model that the children will follow.

You need to think about what the children do with the comments you have written. As a staff you need to think about these questions and address them through your school's marking policy. This should set out ways in which marking can provide constructive feedback to children to help them in their next learning step.

Do they act upon what you have written? Do they have time to act upon it?

Marking can include questions posed by the teacher, setting up a dialogue. These questions should receive an answer and time should be given for this.

> One school adds written questions to the comments in the child's exercise books. The questions are related to the ability and age of the child, focusing on their particular needs.
>
> 'What does the prince look like? Is he handsome? Does he have a horse to ride?'
>
> 'You have used the word "nice" four times in this paragraph. Could you think of three other words you could use instead?'
>
> 'If you were to write a sequel to this story would any of the secondary characters appear again? What new characters might you introduce?'
>
> 'This was a super story until I reached the part about the cat disappearing. Then it seemed to fade away. Can you look again at that last paragraph? Do you think you could add a few sentences to make it more interesting to the reader?'
>
> The children are given time to answer these questions before moving on to the next unit of work.

Do they understand what you have written?

Feedback can also be verbal, but it should still focus specifically on the desired learning outcomes and success criteria that were set for that area of the curriculum. Encouraging dialogue with the child or with a group of children will help you to see whether the child has understood your marking. It also can be a chance to respond to the questions you have posed for weak readers/writers. This can be done with a teaching assistant, as long as she fully understands what the marking meant and where it fits into the children's targets.

How improving the marking can be of benefit

The results of implementing a marking policy for one school have been very positive.

- This system of marking has cut down on marking time.
- Assessments are focused on the learning objectives set for the lesson.

Do they read the comments? Can they read the comments?

> One school decided that feedback to younger children would be mainly verbal but that a written comment would be recorded in their books related to the learning intention. For example, a comment such as, 'Well done Sophie, you have used full stops well' would be put in the book while the teacher would ask one or two questions of the child to ensure that the required learning had taken place.

Using symbols rather than words reduces the time that the teacher spends writing out his or her marking, but also enables non-readers or weak readers to access the information independently. Use only a limited number of symbols with the youngest children. As the children move through the classes new ones can be added to the list as necessary to match the needs of the work involved.

> One school decided that the many symbols used in marking needed to be standardised, and therefore produced a table of symbols and their uses for common use within the school. This had value, not only in that children understood the marking more easily but it also meant that they didn't need to learn a new set of symbols each time they changed teachers.

The Assessment Handbook

- This type of marking has also proved useful in providing a diagnostic tool in the record of achievement for each child.
- The children's books have become an assessment record.
- This type of marking has also allowed the teachers to track the results of the associated learning outcomes which then feed into the future planning process.
- Children receive focused feedback that helps them to understand what they have achieved and what the next learning step will be, so they are involved in the learning process.
- Any problems encountered by children are noted and this feeds into future planning.
- Above all, the marking and feedback to children are consistent and based on evidence found in their work. Following on from this, children started giving each other feedback, which was accurate and focused.

Making your marking more effective

As we have established, marking has to be effective if it is to help with the assessment process. Below is a list of important points that you should consider if your marking is to be effective.

EFFECTIVE MARKING
- Is consistent with school policy
- Provides feedback to children
- Is both oral and written
- Is shared with parents
- Focuses on learning objectives
- Influences future learning opportunities
- Gives opportunities for child feedback
- Recognises achievement and future learning

Figure 1

Marking has to be consistent and follow the school's assessment, recording and reporting policy

Children need consistency to be able to benefit fully from marking. Changes of teacher should have little impact if the school's marking policy is applied consistently.

Children should be able to learn from the comments you write and questions posed to them, both orally and in their workbooks. Children will learn to trust these comments, to know whether they have achieved the learning intentions and face the next stage of learning with confidence.

Any questions you pose should be differentiated, taking into account the level of learning and the ability of the child. For example, at one level a child may be asked to multiply two numbers by counting on while at another level they may be asked to calculate the answer mentally.

Written marking should use the agreed symbols (detailed in the school policy document) so that all children can access your comments independently.

Marking has to provide feedback to children about their work promptly and regularly

Children need regular feedback in order to gain a purposeful understanding of their strengths, weaknesses and the next stage of learning. This needs to happen on a regular basis so that the marking relates to learning that is fresh in the child's mind.

For example, in the plenary session of a literacy lesson, the teacher can focus on the learning intention and use a range of questions to determine whether the whole class, a group or an individual have understood. The teacher can then scrutinise the child's workbooks, providing questions specifically suited to that child.

For the marking and feedback to be effective, it needs to be delivered as soon as possible, and certainly, the questions need to be in the children's workbooks so that they can consider them at the beginning of the next lesson and be prepared for the next stage of learning.

Marking should include both oral and written feedback as appropriate

As we have seen previously, marking should be a mix of both oral and written feedback. Sometimes oral feedback can be delivered to the whole class, sometimes to a group of children but mainly to individual children.

Written feedback is almost always individual and relates to the specific abilities of that child. Teachers may think that this is unrealistic from a time point of view but, if done thoughtfully, it will actually save you time. For example, by focusing on the specific learning objective, marking can be directed, thus saving time.

Oral feedback can be given by targeting individuals and small groups. This doesn't all have to happen in one day but can be planned so that every child receives this type of feedback over the course of a week. Of course, those children who are having difficulty in achieving a particular learning outcome will need more focused feedback more often. But we also need to remember that children who have achieved the learning outcome need that feedback too so that they can move on to the next stage of learning with confidence.

Marking should focus on the learning objectives and criteria for success

For any marking to be relevant, it needs to be focused on the learning objectives for the lesson and their consequent criteria for success. Teachers sometimes find themselves in something of a dilemma when faced with children's workbooks. They see errors in the work and want to correct everything in them. Not only is this time-consuming, it can also be demoralising to the child faced with a page covered with symbols and not knowing what to correct first. By focusing only on the learning objectives for that particular lesson, you can give very unambiguous feedback which the child can immediately learn from while spending less time on the marking of the work. You may note patterns in children's mistakes for future lesson planning.

Teachers should provide children with opportunities to assess their own and each other's work and give feedback

Not all marking and feedback need to be teacher-directed. Black and Wiliam (1998) observe that

> 'pupils can only assess themselves when they have a sufficiently clear picture of the targets that their learning is meant to attain. Surprisingly, and sadly, many pupils do not have such a picture, and appear to have become accustomed to receiving classroom teaching as an arbitrary sequence of exercises with no overarching rationale … When pupils do acquire such an overview, they then become more committed and more effective as learners: their own assessments become an object of discussion with their teachers and with one another, and this promotes even further that reflection on one's own ideas that is essential to good learning.'

QCA (2001) endorses this view.

> 'Learners should be helped to develop the capacity and the habit of self reflection so that they can increasingly become self-monitoring and self-regulating.'

Teachers should ensure that children understand their achievements and know what they have to do next to make progress

It is important that learning outcomes are made explicit to children. This allows them to know when they have achieved them. Good marking will then lead the child into the next stage of learning. Stobart and Gipps (1997) make the point that by enabling children to do this you avoid competition with others by focusing on your own needs.

> 'Metacognition is the process of being aware of one's own learning: good learners monitor their learning and thinking processes through self-monitoring. It focuses the pupil's evaluation on his or her own performance rather than in comparison with others, which we know is more likely to maintain motivation.'

Teachers should use the information gained, together with other information, to adjust future learning plans

When marking, both orally and in children's workbooks, you receive a vast amount of information about what the children are learning. You should be using this information to adjust or modify future planning to take account of possible gaps in skills or knowledge.

> When marking a piece of historical writing, the teacher finds that the children have achieved the learning objective set but notices that many of the children have not used capital letters accurately. She decided to adjust her planning to re-visit the use of capital letters in a future literacy lesson.

This information can also be used to ensure differentiation in the classroom, using the teacher's observations when marking to plan work for different groups of children.

The school should share the policy with parents so they can reinforce it

Successful schools often view education as a partnership between them and parents. The new Ofsted framework for inspecting schools places a much greater emphasis on parental views of the school. Sharing the school's marking policy with parents, through a curriculum evening for example, is desirable for several reasons. There is then a shared understanding of how the school assesses children's work. Parents will be given opportunities to understand how the work is marked, which will be different from the marking they were subjected to at school. Parents will gain an understanding that not every mistake will be corrected and see that marking is developmental, leading on to the next stage of learning.

MARKING FEEDBACK CHECKLIST

	1	2	3	4
4 - mirrors the statement 3 - room for minor improvements 2 - elements require development 1 - requires re-thinking				
Regular and prompt marking happens in all subjects in my class.				
The marking process includes both written and verbal feedback.				
Marking focuses on the learning intentions as a criterion for success.				
Children are provided with opportunities to assess their own and others' work.				
Marking strategies help children understand what they have achieved and what they need to do next.				
I use the outcomes of marking, along with other information, to adjust future teaching plans.				

Based on a grid by S Clarke – Primary Assessment Practice: Evaluation and Development Materials

Parents have a role to play when helping their children at home. They can concentrate on the teacher's learning objectives and support their children in a more focused way.

The school should regularly review the policy, making sure that it is understood by new members of staff

The marking policy should be reviewed annually. It may be that nothing needs to be changed, but reviewing the policy annually allows discussion and debate which is necessary in order to make sure that the policy is still current. This also has importance when new members of staff join the school. It helps to clarify anything that is unclear to a new teacher and allows them to become part of the revision process thus gaining ownership.

In conclusion

Focused marking is a vital tool in ongoing teacher assessment, allowing the opportunity to ensure that learning is broken down into easily manageable units of work, each with their own set of learning intentions. By marking to these learning intentions, by praising achievement and asking pertinent questions we can ensure that they are met and understood by children in our classrooms.

So remember…

1. It is important to ensure that the school has a consistent and well-structured policy for marking with agreed symbols and methodology.

2. Marking can be both oral and written, making use of questioning skills to discover areas where learning has taken place and areas still needing development.

3. Marking should be closely related to the learning objectives set for the lesson.

4. Marking has to provide feedback to children about their work, promptly and regularly.

5. You should provide children with opportunities to assess their own and each other's work and give feedback.

6. You should ensure that children understand their achievements and know what they have to do next to make progress.

7. You should use the information gained together with other information to adjust future learning plans.

8. The school should share the policy with parents so they can reinforce it.

9. The school should regularly review the policy, making sure that it is understood by new members of staff, so that practice continues to reflect school policy.

A SAMPLE MARKING POLICY

Introduction

This policy is concerned with the way in which we mark children's work. It aims to develop a consistent approach to marking throughout the school.

Aims

- To motivate children to want to produce high quality work.
- To teach children to recognise what they do well.
- To help children to improve through the setting of challenging but achievable targets.
- To allow children to build a picture of their strengths and weaknesses by giving quality feedback.
- To foster an ethos where it is acceptable to make mistakes as long as learning then allows children to remedy them.
- To establish a consistent approach to the way work is marked so that children understand how and why their work is marked.

The marking process

Before a piece of work is undertaken, children should be clear what is going to be assessed when the work is marked (Learning Intention).

During a piece of work, over-marking should be avoided. It is more realistic that a child will benefit from the targeting of key learning points related to the learning intention set.

After a piece of work, a comment may be written. Comments should be motivational and personal. While single word comments have their place, ideally time should be found to

- write a brief comment that praises something within the piece of work, no matter how small
- ask questions that target a specific area for improvement.

Before the next piece of work is undertaken, time will be given to re-visit the targets from the previous piece of work.

Approaches to marking

Marking should be undertaken as quickly as possible, ideally *with* the child/a group, so that dialogue can take place and areas of difficulty can be dealt with promptly.

Selective self-marking by older children is acceptable providing the accuracy of marking is checked and initialled by the teacher afterwards.

Marks awarded at the end of a piece of work have their place but should not dominate. Children should be taught to reflect on, and respond effectively to, teacher comments.

Correcting every mistake can be demoralising.

When written comments are made by staff, questions should be posed which children should be expected to answer.

Time should be allowed for children to reflect on teachers' written comments.

Teachers should write legibly and model good practice.

Review

To be reviewed by the staff, headteacher and Curriculum and Assessment Committee of the governing body on a two-yearly cycle.

Next review date: Spring 2005

School marking key

sp	Spelling error
p	Punctuation error
exp	Error in expression of Standard English
//	New paragraph

7 The assessment of skills

Within each subject area of the curriculum there are two aspects of learning – knowledge and skills. Across the whole of education there are skills that children need to develop to enable them to become life-long learners – skills such as thinking, problem-solving and research skills. This chapter deals with the skills children are acquiring and how you can assess them.

In this chapter there is information on

- curriculum-based skills
- identifying other learning skills
- planning to teach learning skills.

This chapter contains practical strategies for

- assessing learning skills
- assessing 'I can…'
- assessing the process, not just the product
- assessing achievements in practical subjects.

Curriculum-based skills

These can be simply described as 'I can do…' (as opposed to 'I know…'). These skills start in simple ways in the Foundation Stage classes and progress as children mature and their experiences widen They are also cross-curricular in many instances.

A primary school with 300 children on role wanted to list the key skills children used in history. They used half of an INSET day to do this.

Before the session the coordinator set out broad headings for the skills which he presented to the staff at the start of this activity.

- Use historical vocabulary.
- Use research skills to gather information.
- Use evidence from the past and interpret it.
- Use secondary sources of information.
- Use ICT to retrieve and communicate information.

The staff took one of these skills at a time, and all staff then contributed to make a chronological list of the development of this skill, from the least able child in the Foundation Stage to the highest-achieving child in Year 6.

They used an interactive whiteboard on which to record the development. This meant that they could move skills up or down the list, add in new ideas and so on while keeping the work easy to read.

Note This can be a time-consuming activity, so if you decide to do it, keep the pace going. There is a lot to do to cover all the skills.

Keep checking back with any resources you already use. You may be able to 'lift' some ideas and incorporate them into your finished list.

Their next task was to divide the lists of skills into approximate age bands – each band being the skills that they expected the average child in Reception, Year 2, Year 6… to be able to do. (Some of the children in each year group will obviously be working at a lower level, while others will be achieving skills assigned to later year groups.)

Identifying other learning skills

There are skills that children need to develop if they are to become independent learners. These include skills in the areas of questioning, thinking and researching. Children also need to be able to solve problems for themselves. These skills are integral to the process of carrying out the self-assessment that we want our children to be able to do. They can't always be taught as individual elements, but will form part of the tasks you set the children across the curriculum. In your planning you need to identify when and where this learning will take place. You could indicate this simply by an initial letter placed next to the appropriate activities.

But how will you know the children's current level of development in these areas? How will you know when children have developed any of these skills? In the same way as you identified the average child's progression through the curriculum skills, you need to identify the potential route through the acquisition and development of learning skills.

Planning to teach learning skills

Once you know the route that the child will follow, you can plan to include it in your teaching. Some of these aspects you will recognise as part of the literacy programme, and some form part of the history and ICT programmes. You will be teaching them specifically. Look through your copy of the National Curriculum and highlight the aspects of the programmes that are linked to the development of learning skills. Look at the school's medium-term plans or the QCA schemes of work, and do the same. You should be able to find lots of opportunities to teach aspects of these skills in what you are already doing.

For other aspects you will need to think of suitable activities for the children to carry out. There are some interesting ideas for developing thinking skills in Edward De Bono's book *Teach Your Child How to Think* (Penguin Books) that can be adapted for classroom use. They will fit into your work for speaking and listening, for PSHE or for those odd

---

When a small village infant school looked at this aspect of their planning, they brainstormed all the possible steps for questioning and research skills, and then placed them in the order they felt that their children passed through.

Questioning skills

- Can respond to closed questions.
- Recognises the who, why, what, etc., words.
- Can set closed questions with support/independently.
- Can respond to higher-order questions.
- Recognises structures such as what do you think…, how do you think…, why do you imagine that…
- Knows that some questions don't have a 'right' answer.
- Can set open-ended questions with support/independently.

Research skills

- Knows the difference between fiction and non-fiction texts.
- Recognises headings, key words, etc., as elements of non-fiction texts.
- Can scan text for key words.
- Can use an index/table of contents in texts.
- Can use key word search in ICT.
- Can observe artefacts and make deductions about their use, origin, etc., with support/independently.
- Can read two texts with conflicting information and discuss their merits.
- Can make a judgement/come to a decision in discussion with others, taking account of all the available evidence.

five minutes when you are waiting for everyone to tidy away at the end of a session. You could try hot-seating to develop questioning skills, or set up a small display consisting of a strange object or an 'ancient' manuscript and a flipchart on which the children can write their thoughts and opinions. Or they could write down any question that comes to mind about this thing. Leave something there for one day each week and share what is written with the children at the end of the day when you can come to an agreed conclusion about what it is or what it was used for. An alternative to this is to put an everyday object on the display and invite the children to come up with ways in which this object could be used. Try a paper-clip, a peg or a safety pin and look for lateral thinking and weird and wonderful ideas.

You will also need to think about your own presentation style. Do you rely on closed questions? Open-ended questions are harder to devise. You will need to think about them at the planning stage and make notes. As you try them some will be more successful than others. Evaluate their use at the end of the lesson and add a comment to your lesson notes – put a big tick beside the idea that worked or scribble it out if it was totally beyond the children at this stage.

Assessing learning skills

Now that you have identified what the skills are, have some idea of the way they will develop, and know where they fit into your teaching, you will be able to plan to assess the children's development in these areas.

Your assessments will often be through observation. For example, when the children are hot-seating Goldilocks to find out what made her go into an empty cottage in the woods, or the Victorian child who was about to climb his first chimney, you can be observing them.

- Who takes part eagerly, who needs encouragement?
- Who asks closed questions and who asks open-ended ones?
- Who uses information they already have to ask a further question?

Divide the children into small groups. Set them a problem. 'You have been shipwrecked and find yourselves on a deserted island.' Give them a map of the island with key features marked on it. 'Where will you build your camp?' 'Who will be in charge?' 'How will you seek help so that you can be rescued?'

Look for the children's abilities to work as part of a group, to delegate, to listen to each other, to think of the needs of the whole team.

There will be some occasions when you are teaching those aspects that form part of the National Curriculum when you can set a pencil-and-paper exercise for the whole class.

For example, give each child in the group a copy of the same non-fiction text, and a list of questions.

- On which page will you find information about penguins?
- The heading 'All about fins' appears on which page?
- Which sub-heading appears on pages 7, 11 and 14?

Limit the time they have so that you can see whether they are having to read through the whole book or whether they can scan the text for key words.

Set the children a question that they have to answer from the Internet. Ask them to list the route they took to find it. Observe them as they work. Who took the most efficient route? How did they do it?

Include these assessment activities within your planning. Devise a checklist (one for the whole class for each aspect – thinking, questioning, research, problem-solving) on which you can simply tick the names of those children who can demonstrate the required skill on this occasion.

Assessing 'I can...'

Most of the assessments of children's practical skills will take place as they carry out other activities.

- As they make a birthday card in design and technology you can see which of your Reception class children can cut safely, which ones can choose appropriate materials and who can fold paper well.
- Your Year 3 children are studying history and you take in a set of kitchen utensils, some from Victorian times and some from the 1950s. Who can work out what they were used for? Who can identify the materials they are made from and so date them? Who makes a snap judgement? Who weighs up the evidence?
- You take a variety of equipment with you as you go to a local woodland area with your Year 5 children. Who can use the right equipment for the task ahead? Who uses anything that comes to hand? Who makes notes on something they don't recognise so that they can look it up later?

Assessing the process, not just the product

One of the aspects of good teaching is that you should concentrate on the process of learning as much, if not more, than you do on the product. Assessment can help you to see the learning skills in action – or not! There are a number of approaches you can take.

Observe children as they do a piece of work

Use opportunities within your lessons to observe the children as they carry out any task. Think about a piece of handwriting. The child may hand you a piece of work that looks fine. It may be neat and legible, even look as if it was all correctly formed. But when you watch him write, he holds his pencil awkwardly, he starts letters in strange places, he misses out some of the 'joins' and adds them in later. This is not good handwriting. When he needs to write quickly, taking notes, for example, he'll be unable to do it efficiently. Clearly, the process is more important than the product.

Ask the children how they arrived at their answer

This principle applies to all children's work. You need to get inside their mind, to find out their interpretation of the question or the instructions you gave. You need to know the thought processes they go through as they try to resolve the problem. Then you can help them to arrive at a possible solution. This is another part of assessment – finding out how the child arrived at the answer.

A Year 3 class were working on adding two two-digit numbers mentally. David was a particularly able child, ahead of most of the class in most areas of the curriculum despite being a late-August birthday, and the youngest in the class. As a warm-up activity the children had been adding together one one-digit and one two-digit numbers. At this David's hand was always one of the first to go up and any answers that he was asked for were always right. But when faced with both numbers having two-digits he was noticeably slower and not always correct.

The teacher then asked the children to explain how they had arrived at the answer to the last question, 27 and 13. There were many and varied answers, and some children struggled with the language they needed to explain their thought processes, but they were mostly variations on, 'I added the 20 and the 10 and got 30 and then I added the 7 and the 3 and got 10 and then I added the 30 and the 10 and got 40.' But David's answer showed exactly why he was slowing down as the numbers got larger, even though he could accurately calculate much larger numbers on paper. 'I imagined the sum in my head. I could see a picture of it with the 27 at the top and the 13 underneath it and then I added the seven and the three and it made ten and I wrote the zero underneath the three and put the ten on the other side...', and so on. The teacher then spent time with him explaining how paper methods and mental methods needed to be different to be efficient and effective. David struggled with this. The teacher began to understand that here was a little boy whose achievements were due to an ability to learn facts quickly and retain information, and to learn the processes involved in various calculations. However, he wasn't mature enough to adapt his learning methods to different situations, nor could he be flexible in how he tackled his work.

When the teacher 'got inside' David's head she began to understand how his mind worked and therefore how she could help him to progress.

Engage children in a spoken dialogue

Dialogue is another way of finding out how much the child has understood. Sit with a group of children and open up a dialogue. This shouldn't be a question-and-answer session but a two-way conversation when the children are as likely to ask the questions as to answer them. Their questions will let you see where their thinking is going. If it's going in the wrong direction you can gently steer them back to the right path. Be flexible in your own approach to this form of assessment, responding to the children rather than having a predetermined result or answer in your mind.

> 'The dialogue between pupils and a teacher should be thoughtful, reflective, focused to evoke and explore understanding…'
> Black and Wiliam (1998)

When you feed back to individual children as part of your marking process, engage the child in a dialogue about their work. This can be a straightforward way of finding out if the child could develop a certain piece of work as in the following example.

Teacher's comment on Frankie's story – 'You wrote that the monster lived in the cupboard under the stairs. I was wondering how big the monster was. Did it fill the whole cupboard?'

Frankie's reply – 'Yes, it filled every bit of the cupboard.'

Teacher – 'But what about the brushes and things that are usually kept in the cupboard under the stairs?'

Frankie – 'Well, the monster was made of jelly and it could fit round everything in the cupboard.'

Or it could help you to find out about the processes the child went through to get to the answer.

Leon had written in his science report that chocolate doesn't go back to its original form when cooled.

Teacher – 'Did you see what happened to the chocolate when we melted it?'

Leon – 'Yes. It went all runny.'

Teacher – 'And what happened to it when we put the runny chocolate into the fridge?'

Leon – 'It went hard.'

Teacher – 'And how did it start out?'

Leon – 'Hard'

Teacher – 'So it was hard at the start and hard after it had cooled. So isn't that the same?'

Leon – 'No. When it started it was in lots of little squares and when we took it out of the fridge it was just one big lump.'

Use dialogue journals

In the book *Writing with Reason*, edited by Nigel Hall (Hodder and Stoughton), each chapter is an account of approaches that the contributors have used to encourage young children to write. In 'Dear Mrs Duffy', Rose Duffy uses dialogue journals with her Reception class children. In each small book she writes a letter to the child and the child writes a letter back. No help is allowed, and the books are read by the teacher at home, not in the presence of the child – just as when we receive letters in the post. In this instance dialogue journals were used to allow children to develop their own style of writing, but you could try a similar method as part of your assessment programme.

As part of your marking, add a question that demands an answer. Make it open-ended, and let the children know that you will be reading their responses. This response could be followed by a further question at a deeper level. Use this process to explore the way the child is thinking.

The children in Year 5 had written about the destruction of the rainforest. Anna's work was a well-written, factually correct, but rather cold report of the coming of a large company cutting down great swathes of the forest. In the corner of the page she had drawn a small picture of a tree. At the bottom there was a man with a chain saw and at the top was a small bird – with a tear in its eye. This emotion was not present in the writing.

Teacher's comment – 'I was moved by your drawing. I felt so sorry for that little bird that I could hardly concentrate on your written account.'

Anna – 'I wanted to write about the little bird but you said we were to write a report and so I just wrote about things that happened.'

Teacher – 'You can have emotion and feelings in a report. You have to use particular words and phrases to do this.'

Anna was a quiet, self-effacing girl, who was reticent to speak out in a large group. This dialogue enabled a shy child to explain her dilemma.

The teacher then prepared a new lesson for the next day, in which she explored the use of emotive language with the children.

Assessing achievements in practical subjects

Some areas of the curriculum are more difficult to assess in a formal way – music, PE, art and design technology. In primary schools these are essentially practical subjects. There may be end products but it isn't feasible to keep these as evidence of a child's achievements. So how can you assess progress and how can you record what you find out?

Ofsted produce booklets on assessment of these areas, but they concentrate on Key Stages 3 and 4 where children are engaged in written course-work, portfolio collections, etc. They are available on their website, www.ofsted.gov.uk, or through www.ncaction.org.uk. Each one is entitled *Good Assessment Practice in…*

In essence the route to effective assessment is the same integral part of the learning and teaching cycle as for all other areas of the curriculum.

Planning Know what it is you want the children to learn, and how they will do this. Make the tasks challenging but well focused. Ensure differentiation to cater for the needs of all the children. Make sure that each lesson forms part of a cohesive whole.

Learning objectives These need to be clear and precise in your mind and then shared with the children so that they know exactly what you are expecting of them. Help the children to see where this aspect fits into the whole picture.

Observation Watch the children as they carry out the set tasks. How are they using the tools or equipment? Are they conscious of others and the safety of all? Do they keep to the task or do they stray? Are they extending the task or deviating from the work set? Are they working cooperatively, as part of an effective team?

Feedback This will take the place of formal marking of work. Let the children know what they have done well and how/why they achieved this. Encourage them to share in this assessment of their work by allowing them opportunities to learn to evaluate work at different stages of completion, or to reflect on a finished product or composition. Use inclusive phrases such 'How well do you think this is going?' or 'Are you pleased with your ideas so far?' Talk with the children about how they can take their learning forward. Identify the next steps for them. Talk about the development of the skills involved in the activity as well as any product.

Evaluating your planning Any assessment will guide the planning of the next lesson or group of lessons for groups of children or for the class as a whole. Think about the activities that worked well and inspired the children to strive. Note down anything that was less productive, and amend your plans accordingly.

In *Good Assessment Practice in Design and Technology* (Ofsted, 2003) there is a list of the 'effective assessment' practices in D&T departments in secondary schools, followed by the statement

> 'the most significant characteristic is the way in which assessment … is not seen as an end in itself but as a means to improving pupils' achievement … and helping teachers to improve their own teaching programmes.'

A good way to build up your ideas for assessing these practical subjects is to talk with colleagues in other schools, when you can share good practice. Here are a few ideas to start the process. Remember, you can't assess every single aspect of any practical activity. You will have to choose according to the priority of the lesson objective.

Design technology

Every time the children plan and make a finished product, they work through each aspect of the D&T curriculum. You can't assess every aspect at once so make a decision at the planning stage – for example, drawing a plan, testing out a design, joining materials and so on – and assess that aspect only. It is the same as marking the children's work. Ignore the other parts. Concentrate on the specific objective of that lesson and make sure that the children know what this is. Try to assess each aspect at least twice over the school year so that you can monitor progress.

Year 1 Plan then make a pizza topping

- As the children plan, ask them about food choices – do they take account of taste and colour? Do they use appropriate foods? *D&T 1a*

- Look at the completed plans and assess their ability to draw a clear plan (rather than just a picture). Do they add labels or notes on how it will be made? *D&T 1d*

- As the children add the toppings to the ready-made base, assess their ability to use tools safely and appropriately. *D&T 2a*

Year 6 Work in pairs to devise a mechanism for retrieving a heavy stone from a deep container

- As they plan, do they share ideas, take equal responsibility, discuss many options before coming to a decision? *Problem-solving skills*

- Look at the completed plans and assess how useful the plan is for the next stage of the process. Is it accurate? Is it an exploded diagram with labels? Are there lists of materials and tools? Is it feasible? *D&T 1a, 1b, 1c, 1d*

- During the making of the device, do they follow the plan? Do they adapt the plan in response to any difficulties they encounter? *D&T 3a*

Art and design

Year 2 Linked in with their numeracy lessons on symmetry, spatial patterns and relationships, the children are looking at wrapping-paper designs. They then design some of their own.

- Assess their use of colour and pattern. Do they think about combinations of colours, effectiveness of colour for the purpose? *Art 4a*

- As you talk with them about their ideas, can they identify what they like or dislike about their own designs and think how they could improve them? *Art 3a, 3b*

Year 4 As part of their study of the local environment they go for a walk along the High Street. They need to collect visual images to create a collage on their return to school.

- What information do they choose to record? Do they pick key features? Do they reflect the atmosphere of the busy street? *Art 1a, 1b, 1c*

- How do they choose to record this information? Digital photography? Sketches? Collecting materials/rubbings of the textures, etc? *Art 1a, 1b, 1c*

Music

As you assess the children's musical capabilities you should be aware that you will often be looking for an improvement in the quality of the child's performance or response.

- A four-year-old can listen attentively to a piece of music, and so can the child in Year 6. So how will you assess progress? What you can assess is the range of music to which the child will listen attentively. You can talk with them about their response, their feelings or their level of enjoyment. they can start to articulate their preferences and give reasons. They can tell you about the composer's intentions and whether it worked for them. They will have new vocabulary to describe the music. *Music 4a, 4b, 4d*

- You can assess the children's technical abilities. Can they hold the instrument correctly and make it sound in appropriate ways? Can they use it to demonstrate timbre, pitch, etc.? Can they compose on it and play it for others to listen? *Music 1b, 1c, 2b, 4b*

PE

Questioning skills will play a large part in your assessments in PE.

- At the start of a session with your Year 3 children ask them why they need to do warm-up activities. *PE 4b*

- Within your PSHE and science lessons you can discuss with your Year 3 children the need for exercise for health. *PE 4a, 4c*

- Peer assessment is a useful tool when children are doing gymnastics. They can watch one group demonstrating and make useful comments. You will need to model this for the youngest children and talk about the need to respect other people's feelings. *PE 3b*

- Year 2 children can share in creating a large wall picture of a PE lesson, showing the children on different pieces of apparatus. They could write labels about safety, or write a description for each activity. 'When I use the box I have to jump very high to get on it. When I get down I have to land with my knees bent.' *PE 3a, 4b*

The most frequently used assessment tool will be observation. Notice what the children can do, feed back information to the child, and challenge them to try the next step. 'Well done, Sam. You controlled that balance really well. Can you do it again on the other leg?'

So remember...

1. You need to assess the development of children's skills as well as their knowledge.

2. Children need to learn how to learn through the development of skills of questioning, thinking, researching and problem-solving.

3. You need to assess these learning skills and include them in your planning.

4. You can assess children's skills through observation and questioning as they carry out classroom tasks.

5. You should assess the process the child uses as well as the finished product. You can do this through observation, questioning and dialogue with the child.

6. You should be assessing the practical subjects within the curriculum. Plan the assessment activities linked to the specific objectives of the lessons. Use observation and questioning to find out how much the children have understood and to ascertain the level of the skills they have developed.

7. Give children lots of feedback so that they recognise their achievements, their next steps and where this particular learning fits into the whole picture.

8 Assessment and planning

Curriculum planning is an important factor in raising standards in primary schools. In this chapter we are going to consider why good and accurate planning is vitally important and how assessment fits into this process. We will then look at ways in which this planning can be developed, from the school's aims through to individual teacher's plans.

In this chapter there is information on

- why planning is important.

This chapter contains practical strategies for

- making use of planning
- recording your short-term planning.

Why planning is important

'A necessary step in effective planning of both teaching and assessment is to take time to consider the big picture, to establish what will be the curriculum experience of the child as she or he moves through the school from one class to the next ... When the teachers look together at the big picture, they regain the sense that each teacher is making a contribution to the overall learning of the child. To define more clearly the precise nature of that contribution, we now take the big picture and slice it horizontally, to reflect the experiences of a child over a single year.'
(Sutton, 1995)

We need to start by considering the whole structure of planning in the primary school. Most people would agree that successful curriculum planning consists of five interdependent parts. These are

- the school aims
- curriculum policies
- the curriculum map
- school schemes of work
- teaching plans.

The school aims

This is where the broader aims of the school are made explicit and will probably include reference to the school's environment, the support made available to parents, teachers and children, how children are regarded as individuals and relationships between the different parties. Other school aims may refer to things such as a challenging curriculum, each child fulfilling their potential throughout the curriculum, developing lively and enquiring minds, mastering the basic skills and knowledge and the children's awareness of the world around them. We can see that these aims have a direct link to the way the curriculum is planned and delivered.

If these aims are explicit to all then the next step is to ensure that they are reflected in the life and work of the school in practice. This process can be helped by referring to them frequently throughout the whole process of curriculum planning, and by asking questions such as 'How does this reflect the school's aims?', 'What could we do in this curriculum area to reflect the school's aims?', 'Have we taken into account all the aims of the school?'.

Curriculum policies

Curriculum policies should be clear but relatively brief statements, which set out basic principles for that curriculum area. They are unique to a particular school and provide a basis for development. They should be easy to understand and allow anyone coming into the school to understand them and be able to implement them. Curriculum policies should reflect and build on the school's overall aims and should be consistent with each other.

The curriculum map

A curriculum map provides an overview of the school curriculum. It shows how the curriculum will be covered over a period of time. It will be unique to each school, affected by issues such as the size of the school, whether there are mixed-age classes, whether the children are streamed or taught in mixed-ability groups, the number of children with special educational needs and overall levels of attainment. It will also be influenced by the aims of the school and its curriculum policies.

When one school revamped their curriculum map, they included

- clear reference to the National Curriculum, wherever possible, cross-referencing between subjects and identifying ways in which the units of work relate to each other

- identification of where in the curriculum the key skills of literacy and numeracy will be taught

- continuity of skills development

- notional time allocations to each unit

- a monitoring and evaluation plan which detailed responsibilities in monitoring the curriculum.

The curriculum map makes clear what is taught to each year group.

School schemes of work

Once the curriculum map has been devised, the school will need to be more specific about what and how children will learn in each unit of work. Schemes of work are medium-term plans setting out the curriculum for each unit of work.

Schemes of work should detail the following.

- The learning objectives, which are statements about what the children will learn. They need to be clear and concise, specifying what the children will know, understand and be able to do. Good practice tells us that these objectives need to show differentiation, for example 'All children will… Most children will… Some children will…'.

- Activities that children will do in order to achieve the learning objectives.

- The resources needed by the teacher and children when they undertake the activity. This will help teachers to prepare the teaching for particular units of work. This will also help subject coordinators when they undertake a resource audit.

- When and how assessments against the learning objectives will be made. By including these in the scheme of work you can show how the assessments are related to the ongoing learning objectives. It is important to identify the key assessment opportunities where teachers can base assessments on a range of objectives or on particular ones the school feel are important. You don't need to assess against every learning objective. Remember that there will be many opportunities to assess that aren't identified in the scheme of work.

Teaching plans

Teaching plans are the daily or weekly plans that teachers use to deliver the learning objectives and are usually the most detailed of all. Teaching plans take the schemes of work and relate them to the specific classroom situation. You need to take into account what has been achieved and what you need to do to move the children forward. Teaching plans will show specifically the different ability levels within the class and how work will be differentiated accordingly. It is helpful to have a time to evaluate the lessons because it allows you to be reflective about your practice, identifying successful strategies and areas where development is needed. Along with assessments of individuals and groups, this reflection helps with future planning.

The most important principle of curriculum planning is that it should provide a structure for teaching and learning. The focus should be on

- what we want the children to learn (lesson objectives)

- how they will learn it (activities and tasks, presentation and organisation)

- how we will identify successful learning (success criteria, learning outcomes)

- how we will decide what needs to be learned next (assessment of learning).

By linking together the key areas of the curriculum planning, a structure can be established that does all of these things.

> 'The provision of activities at the right level of demand and setting appropriate expectations is the prerequisite for learning. This "getting in the right ballpark" is an important part of planning class activities, which has been called macro-matching. Children are individual … so for each to have the opportunity to learn there needs to be a closer matching at the individual level. This "micro-matching" … depends upon the teacher's knowledge.'
> (Harlen, 1993, p95)

A checklist to enable you to consider issues relating to your weekly planning

My planning

☐ contains clear specific learning intentions for assessment

☐ takes into account prior knowledge, skill and understanding that the children bring to the learning situation

☐ takes into account a range of learning styles

☐ recognises that all learning does not need to be assessed

☐ recognises that unanticipated learning occurs

☐ identifies what will be assessed for children or groups, how this will be done and who will do it.

Making use of planning

Assessment is an inextricable part of planning. If planning is good it forms a foundation for quality learning.

Medium-term plans are standard plans because they need to remain constant over a number of years to ensure continuity and progression. They may contain some suggested activities, but these should be optional and teachers will need to change these in their short-term plans to meet the needs of their current cohort of children. The choice of activity can then be directly related to the needs of the children as determined by ongoing assessments both by the teacher and the children.

Short-term planning is focused on learning intentions and the needs of each particular cohort or group of children. With the learning intentions clearly identified, the next point to consider is how the children will demonstrate their learning/understanding. Once this is decided, appropriate activities can be designed that will meet the needs of the children. This is where teacher creativity is so important. When we challenge children in an effective way they are more likely to achieve that learning intention.

> 'Our long- and medium-term plans don't change too much. We no longer spend copious amounts of time writing and re-writing these plans. We now concentrate on our short-term plans. This is where we ensure that we have specific learning intentions, often but not exclusively taken from our medium-term plans. We also ensure that the work is differentiated according to the abilities of the children and possible assessment opportunities are identified.'

Recording your short-term planning

You may be in a school where the teachers all use an agreed planning format. Or you have the freedom to write your plans out in your own preferred style. Whichever way, you will have certain key headings.

You will need to identify

- the specific objective of the lesson and reference any National Curriculum documents or literacy and numeracy schemes

- the way in which you will introduce this to the children

- the activities you will do with the whole class

- the activities for each group, showing differentiation

- the plenary session when you will draw together the learning and relate back to the lesson objective

- assessment opportunities.

For each aspect of the lesson it is a good idea to note down the expected time allocation so that you can see how the lesson will progress and how much emphasis you will place on each aspect.

> 'Our short-term plans are usually completed weekly although, at times, we find that this is too long-term for us! We are experimenting with plans that are for three days, with the fourth and fifth days added after the first three days, depending on the achievements of the children and where we need to go next. Daily plans are optional for teachers in our school because all the information we need is contained in the weekly plan.'

You can plan to include assessment within any of the four key areas of the lesson. This will depend largely on where the lesson comes in the overall unit of work.

When introducing the work to the children

If this is the first lesson in a unit of work, or even in a section of a unit of work, you will need to assess the children's prior knowledge. Open questioning, mind-mapping and brainstorming activities will enable you to find out where the children are at the moment. It will also help them to find out how much – or how little – they already know about something. Your introduction can then include some indication to the children of how these gaps will be filled and their knowledge and skills extended.

Whole-class teaching/activities
Through your questioning you can get a general picture of how the class is doing or you can plan to focus your

The Assessment Handbook **61**

attention on a chosen group who you think may be struggling or who may be far ahead of the majority.

Group activities You could plan an assessment activity for one of the groups, working with them yourself, completing your records of what they know, how they are progressing or what skills they can now demonstrate.

During the plenary You will be making a broad assessment of the children's progress as they feed back from their group's activity, or respond to your questioning, or give explanations of their thinking.

If you leave room on your short-term planning notes you can add brief comments about these assessments as the lesson finishes. Focused assessments will be recorded in more detail on other records.

At the end of a unit of work you may decide to carry out a whole-class assessment. You may add to the original mind-maps, look again at the brainstorming and add new information. Or it may be a more formal exercise on paper. This may take the main part of your lesson, replacing the whole-class and group activities. Make sure this is clearly marked in your plans. Allow time for it. Think about how you will introduce it to the children and how you will bring the lesson to a close. Also plan time to feedback to the children how well they have done, and talk with them about where they will go next. Fix the assessment and the learning into the whole picture.

When you revisit this curriculum area make sure that you look back over your plans, read through the comments that you made and the details about individual children. Then start off your next round of planning, building on from where this group of children actually left off – not where the medium-term planning assumes them to be.

> 'For assessment to function formatively, the results have to be used to adjust teaching and learning…'
> Black and Wiliam (1998)

Assessing your own lesson is also worth doing.

- Award yourself a tick for activities that worked well, achieved your teaching objectives and allowed the children to learn as planned.

- Two ticks could mean that the children engaged well in the activity.

- If things didn't go well, put a cross next to the part of the lesson that didn't meet your expectations and try to think why. Make a note of this against the medium-term planning when you have a chance, so that you can think about it further, or ask colleagues for their ideas as to how you can teach this aspect more effectively.

So remember…

1 Planning is an important aspect in raising curriculum standards.

2 Planning can only be effective if clear learning intentions are present and good use of assessment information is made to develop the learning intentions in future lessons.

3 Good planning provides a framework within which teachers can devise their own teaching programmes to deliver specific learning intentions, based on the knowledge they gained through their assessment of the children.

> 'What really makes a difference to children's progress is the day to day work of being absolutely certain where children are now and where they need to go next and how quickly on an individual level.'
> (NAHT, 2000)

Example of a scheme of work

The section 'prior learning' will pinpoint areas for assessment at the start of the unit of work.
The section 'expectations' will pinpoint the areas for assessment at the end of the unit of work.

SAINT SEBASTIAN'S CHURCH OF ENGLAND (AIDED) PRIMARY SCHOOL		ART	
Unit 1A	SELF-PORTRAIT		Term: Autumn (1st half)

ABOUT THE UNIT
In this unit, children make a self-portrait to communicate ideas about themselves. They talk about images of children in drawings, paintings and photographs and artists' self-portraits in order to develop ideas about how they will portray themselves. They investigate a range of drawing materials and techniques and learn how to mix and use colour in a painting.

WHERE THE UNIT FITS IN
This unit builds on Unit 1A 'Ourselves' and links with Unit 2C 'Variation' in the science scheme of work. It also links with personal, social and health education (PSHE) when children learn about respecting the differences and similarities between people.

WHAT THE UNIT COVERS

Art	Shape
Craft	Form
Design	Space
2D	Painting
3D	Collage
Individual work	Textiles
Collaborative work	Digital media
Line	Sculpture
Tone	Print making
Colour	Texture
Pattern	

VOCABULARY
In this unit children will have an opportunity to use words and phrases related to
- lines, eg. thin, bold, feint, wavy, broken
- colours, eg. bright, dull, light, dark
- colour mixing, eg. thick, thin, watery, blending bright and dull, and light and dark colours
- shapes, eg. long, oval, curvy
- textures, eg. smooth, crinkly, rough
- composition in a drawing or painting, eg. arranging, visual qualities.

RESOURCES
For practical work.
- Drawing materials, eg. soft graphite pencils (2B and 4B), willow, charcoal, soft pastels, oil pastels, wax crayons.
- Painting materials, eg. block, powder or liquid paint, large, medium and small bristle paint brushes.
- Dressing-up clothes.
- Mirrors.

Suggested examples of art, craft and design.
- Images of children in a range of media, including photographs, family albums, advertisements, magazines.
- Portraits by different artists, eg. 'John Friedrich the magnanimous at the age of six' by Lucas Cranach the Elder, 'Two little girls' by Isaac Oliver, 'The little dancer' by Edgar Degas, 'Self-portrait in a straw hat' by Vigée-Lebrun, 'The painter and his pug' by William Hogarth.

EXPECTATIONS
At the end of this unit, most children will be able to

- explore ideas about self-portraits; investigate and use drawing and painting materials and techniques to communicate their ideas about themselves in a self-portrait; say what they think and feel about their own and others' work; suggest ways of improving their own work

Some children will not have made so much progress. They will be able to

- use drawing and painting techniques to communicate ideas about themselves in a self-portrait; talk about what they think or feel about their own work.

Some children will have progressed further. They will be able to

- collect visual and other information to help them develop their work; investigate visual and tactile qualities of media; make a self-portrait showing their ideas about themselves; comment on similarities and differences in their own and others' work; adapt and improve their own work.

PRIOR LEARNING
It is helpful if children have
- explored ideas about themselves
- used drawing media and worked from observation
- talked about their drawings and paintings as they develop
- looked at other artists' work and talked about what they think or feel about it.

FUTURE LEARNING
In Unit 2A 'Picture this!', children explore an issue or event in their own lives and record their observations and ideas using a variety of media.

ADAPTING THE UNIT OF WORK
Children could
- represent themselves by selecting and making an arrangement of the objects that they value, eg. toys, clothes, books, games, recording their observations and making a painting
- investigate mark-making using ICT tools, including flood fill and spray tools. They could use these effects to make portraits showing feelings such as anger, fear or joy, building on Unit 2B 'Creating pictures' in the ICT scheme of work
- explore the shape and form of the head, using self-hardening clay to model in three dimensions, and use their sculptures as a starting point for developing large-scale expressive portrait paintings (see *Expectations in Art at Key Stages 1 and 2*, 'Faces and Heads', p14, SCAA 1997).

The Assessment Handbook

Example of a medium term teaching plan

The section 'learning outcomes' will pinpoint areas for assessment

LEARNING OBJECTIVES Children should learn	TEACHING ACTIVITIES	LEARNING OUTCOMES Children can	POINTS TO NOTE
EXPLORING AND DEVELOPING IDEAS			
• about differences and similarities in the work of artists	• Talk about selected images of children, raising questions about the ways in which the clothes worn, the pose and the activities shown, convey ideas about the children. • Talk about selected self-portraits focusing on how artists have conveyed ideas about themselves, eg. how do the artists show themselves? As a painter? As a mother? As a friend? As a person with status? Ask the children to suggest why portraits are made, eg. to record an important time in a person's life, to project a powerful image of the person, to portray individuals as wealthy, knowledgeable or hard working.	• identify differences in ways that children are represented in art • identify ways in which artists represent themselves and suggest reasons for this	• Ask the children to collect photographs and other information about themselves at home, school and play. • Display images of children by painters, photographers and illustrators (including photographs of the children in the class) together with examples of artists' self-portraits.
• to ask and answer questions about the starting points for their work, and to develop their ideas	• Focus the children's attention on one self-portrait. Ask them to describe – the person or people and the objects they are holding, wearing, etc. (the content, subject) – the main shapes and colours, etc. in the image (the visual elements and the composition) – how the image is made – is it a photograph? a painting? a print? (materials and processes used) – how the image makes them feel about the person portrayed – what sort of person is this? what is the person doing? what does the image tell you about the person? (the ideas and meanings). • Ask the children to look at each other's appearance, eg. their height, shape, colour of skin and hair, facial features. Talk about how the children would show themselves in a portrait. What clothes would they be wearing? How would they like to be seen? What would they be doing? Would they include objects such as toys or a pet?	• identify aspects of one self-portrait and say what they think and feel about it • identify ways in which children in the class are similar to and different from each other • suggest ideas about how to represent themselves	• Develop strategies to give children confidence to talk about the work of artists. These could include focusing attention on one image and asking one or more children to adopt the pose of the sitter in the portrait, or using dressing-up clothes to replicate a portrait. • Links with National Literacy Strategy: Framework for teaching, Year 1 vocabulary extension, where children learn new words from shared experiences. • Links with Unit 1A 'Ourselves' and Unit 2C 'Variation' in the science scheme of work where children learn about the similarities and differences between humans. It could also link to PSHE by helping children to learn to respect similarities and differences between people.
INVESTIGATING AND MAKING			
• to investigate the possibilities of a range of materials and processes, including drawing	• Ask the children to investigate a range of drawing media and the marks they can make, eg. try out techniques for showing textures of hair, smoothness of skin, pattern on clothing. • Encourage children to explore different types of marks, eg. bold, expressive, quiet, wriggly. Ask them to use marks that communicate ideas about themselves and how they would like to be seen by others, eg. big and bold, quiet and thoughtful.	• experiment with and use drawing media and techniques to create a range of visual effects	• Explain that the purpose of the activity is to learn about different drawing media, and to investigate different kinds of marks and how they might be used in their work. It is not to produce a finished drawing.

LEARNING OBJECTIVES Children should learn	TEACHING ACTIVITIES	LEARNING OUTCOMES Children can	POINTS TO NOTE
INVESTIGATING AND MAKING			
• to try out tools and techniques and apply these to materials and processes, including drawing	• Give the children mirrors. Ask them to look at themselves and think about the size and shape of their faces and about the size of parts of their face or body in relation to each other. • Ask them to draw life-size and miniature self-portraits, including themselves as a whole or just their head and shoulders.	• record self-portraits from observation, working on different scales	• Teach children how to organise their workspace, including setting out and packing away materials. Encourage children to think about how to use tools and materials safely and effectively.
• to review what they have done	• Display children's work to show how they look different from one another. Put the images of children they talked about earlier alongside their work and talk about similarities and differences. Reinforce that the children can choose how to project themselves in their self-portraits, and show themselves as they wish to be seen.	• comment on differences in others' work	• Encourage children to experiment with mixing colour and with controlling the consistency of the paint. Show them how to apply the colour in stages, deciding which parts they will treat as flat colour and which parts they will work on and make more complex.
• to represent observations, ideas and feelings, and design and make a painting	• Using their drawings as a reference, ask the children to make a larger painting. Ask them to draw the outline and main shapes of the portrait using light-coloured chalk or a medium brush and a light colour. Show them how to mix paint and colour to represent skin, eyes, hair, etc. Demonstrate a system of colour mixing, eg. combining two colours to achieve a range, adding black or white to make darker or lighter tones.	• plan, compose and make a self-portrait painting	• Provide opportunities for children to discuss their plans and think through the ideas they would like to convey.
EVALUATING AND DEVELOPING WORK			
• to review what they and others have done and say what they think and feel about it	• As a class, review the children's drawings and paintings and the decisions they made. Talk about what they think has been most successful. What ideas about themselves and meanings did they want to convey? How have they represented themselves? What have they included in the portrait and why? What are they doing in their portrait? How have they used the media – drawing, paint? How have they used visual qualities such as line, colour, texture? What do they think about the techniques they have used?	• use descriptive and expressive vocabulary to talk about their portrait work	• Displaying children's work can be part of the review process. It gives children the opportunity to compare their work with that of others in the class and can help them to learn from their successes as well as from their mistakes and difficulties.
• to identify what they might change in their current work or develop in their future work.	• Ask the children to say what they would like to change about their work and what they think they would like to do in the future. How might they show themselves differently? What characteristics might they have portrayed instead? What would they like to show in a portrait of someone else?	• identify the successful parts of their painting and explain why they think these parts are successful • identify what they might like to change or improve.	

The Assessment Handbook

EXAMPLE OF PLANNING FORMATS FOR WEEKLY PLANNING

WEEKLY PLANNING SHEET

Teacher:		Year group(s):		Term:	W/e:
Subject:	Learning intentions	Activities/Resources	Differentiation	Assessment	Evaluation
Literacy					
Numeracy					
Science					

WEEKLY PLANNING SHEET

Subject:	Learning intentions	Activities/Resources	Differentiation	Assessment	Evaluation
ICT					
Design Technology					
History					
Geography					
Art					
Music					
Physical Education					
Religious Education					

9 Involving children in their own assessment

Good teaching has always involved the children in the learning and assessment process. This has meant that ways have to be found to inform and involve the learners themselves in the process of assessment, not just on what they have achieved but also in determining what the next steps to learning may be.

In this chapter there is information on

- why we should involve children
- the effect of self-esteem on learning
- what is involved in self-assessment
- how to encourage children to share in the programme.

This chapter contains practical strategies for

- how to promote child self-assessment
- techniques you can use in your classroom.

Why we should involve children

In *Inside the Black Box*, Black and Wiliam (1998) say

> '…pupils can only achieve a learning goal if they understand that goal and can assess what they need to achieve it. So self-assessment is essential to learning.'

Involving children in the assessment of their work has long-term benefits in the learning process with benefits for both children and teachers. There must, however, be a commitment and belief that the self-assessment process actually works.

Benefits for children include the following.

- They can take a greater sense of responsibility for their own learning by knowing what they have to achieve and the success criteria for each learning step.
- They can recognise the next stage in their learning by careful planning.
- They feel more secure about making mistakes because the classroom culture recognises that often new learning follows.
- Self-esteem is raised as a result, culminating in a more positive approach to solving problems.
- They feel more involved in the learning process, being part of the learning process and not a passive recipient. This leads to increased independence, interdependence and motivation with a far more effective focus on learning.

The following are some of the advantages for teachers.

- There is a shift of responsibility for learning from the teacher to the child, with lessons becoming more productive and a marked decrease in distraction.
- They can identify child progress more accurately and, therefore, match the next learning step more precisely to children's needs.
- Their questioning skills may improve, allowing them to differentiate work more effectively and provide greater challenge for the children.
- As children become more adept at explaining how they have learned, teachers can identify the thought processes of the children and thus build on those processes.

The National Curriculum Handbook, page 21, tells us that

> 'The key skill of improving their own learning and performance involves pupils reflecting on and critically evaluating their own work and what they have learnt, and identifying ways to improve their learning and performance.'

The effect of self-esteem on learning

Children who succeed are in a more favourable position to learn from their next experience. Conversely, children who feel that they have failed can become locked into a cycle of failure. There are many ways of tackling this within our classrooms, to break the cycle and help children review their own self-image. Many of these were dealt with in the pfp book *The Positive Behaviour Handbook*.

The effect of self-esteem on the learning process cannot be underestimated. You can change the culture in your classroom by encouraging the children to see difficulty as part of the learning process, thus counteracting the fear of failure. Getting all the answers right quickly and easily is no longer seen as praiseworthy. In fact, the opposite is true, it's a sign that little has been learned.

> 'Making mistakes, struggling to understand and asking for help are all seen as signs of the learning process with pupils receiving praise for showing that they are learning … In this type of classroom climate, high attaining pupils are more willing to admit difficulties and lower attaining pupils begin to understand that they are not essentially different from their "clever" peers. Learning is hard; it's about feeling uncertain; it's about taking risks and it's the same for everyone.'
> (AAIA, *Self-Assessment*, p8)

This can happen when children are involved in the assessment of their own work. They know their own broad target, they know the specific objective of the lesson and the task they have completed, and they can rate their own learning against these criteria. They can see when they have moved closer to their target even if they haven't reached it yet. By adopting this sort of culture in the classroom, you are raising children's self-esteem and helping them become more effective learners.

What is involved in self-assessment?

Research shows us that there are certain important elements that you can use in your classroom to encourage children in assessing their work.

- Share the learning objectives for the lesson with the children and make them explicit.
- Give the children time to reflect on what learning has taken place and how the learning has been effective.
- Encourage the children to self-assess their work before handing it to you.
- Create a positive learning climate in the classroom in which making errors is seen as a positive outcome allowing improvement, not a sign of failure.
- Develop individual target-setting, incorporating curriculum targets into discussions with children.
- Support the children to recognise the next steps and share the criteria that outline the standards that they are striving to achieve.
- Experiment with feedback techniques that support, motivate and enable your children to improve.

Of course, all these elements are interlinked. By sharing the learning objectives and having clear curriculum targets, you are enabling the children to understand just what it is they are trying to learn or practise. By giving positive and informative feedback you will enable children to decide the next steps in their learning. Being confident that progress can be achieved is essential to allow risks to be taken.

Self-assessment by children is not a hand-over of responsibility from teacher to child, but rather, an essential element if children are to begin to take responsibility for their own learning.

How to encourage children to share in the programme

Assessment is part of the learning cycle. By inviting children to play their part in the assessment programme you are encouraging them to share responsibility for their learning. You can give them practical strategies to help them to assess their learning, to mark their work or gauge their level of attainment, but first you must create the right climate within your classroom. This can be the most important element in involving your children as partners in learning. For child self-assessment to be successful you have to create a climate that is conducive to effective learning, that is, to embrace honesty, openness and no fear of failing.

Be wary of creating a climate in which only success matters, where praise is directed only to the children who attain, rather than to those who strive and work hard. When only top marks and answering questions are celebrated, your high-attaining children may be developing a positive self-image but are not necessarily learning as much as they are capable of. At the same time, lower-attaining children suffer constant failure and the consequent effect on their self-esteem.

The Association of Assessment Inspectors and Advisors (AAIA), in their report on *Self-Assessment*, page 7, tell us that

> 'Pupils, who believe they can learn, face new challenges in a state of "relaxed alertness", an optimum state to take risks and learn. Success reinforces self-esteem and the cycle is complete. Low attaining pupils, who believe they cannot learn, experience stress when facing a new challenge. This causes "emotional flooding" when all they can think about is how to get out of the situation – a flight response – and hence no learning takes place. In each case, there is feedback that amplifies the output, so self-esteem – negative or positive – grows with each repetition of the cycle.'

How to promote pupil self-assessment

The building bricks

The first thing that needs to happen is that there is a change in culture within the classroom. This will be a slow and gradual process with lots of small, planned changes taking place over a period of time. This is very much a teacher-led process, within the guidelines of the school. Combined with this is ensuring that children are clear about what they are learning. Obviously, for children to be able to understand the learning intentions, the teacher has to be clear first. Careful planning is the key here but don't plan in detail too far ahead, as you may have to refine your planning.

Self-assessment strategies

According to the AAIA, to enable child self-assessment to support learning effectively, there are six things that need to happen within the classroom.

1. There have to be clear success criteria based on the learning intentions, and you need to share this information with the children. This allows children to know what progress they are making and allows the setting of learning targets.

2. You have to use good questioning skills, allowing you to direct the pace of learning in the classroom.

3. You must allow children the opportunity to reflect on the learning that is taking place and also on questions you pose, either written or oral, during the marking process.

4. Try 'pairing' children who can then provide feedback to each other.

5. The use of portfolios provides a record of learning and feedback on the assessment process.

6. You can guide the children in the use of self-assessment through modelling strategies for them.

Child self-assessment

Once these strategies are fully implemented in the classroom, children can become confident about self-assessment and move into independent learning.

Techniques you can use in your classroom

Modelling

Modelling involves using examples of work to help children assess their own work and can be used throughout the teaching and learning process. It can be used at the beginning of a lesson to show children what they need to achieve compared with the lesson objectives. As children develop their thoughts and ideas, they can use the model in order to improve and modify, and when they have completed the work they can compare this with the model to help them identify the success criteria.

Children benefit because they have information about the desired outcome, they can compare their work with a recognised standard, and they can see ways in which they can improve.

Teachers should ensure that

- they make learning intentions clear
- they share the assessment criteria
- they model judgements.

Questioning skills

Teachers use questioning skills to encourage children to think. Try to use more higher-order questioning skills and think about when is the best time to use them.

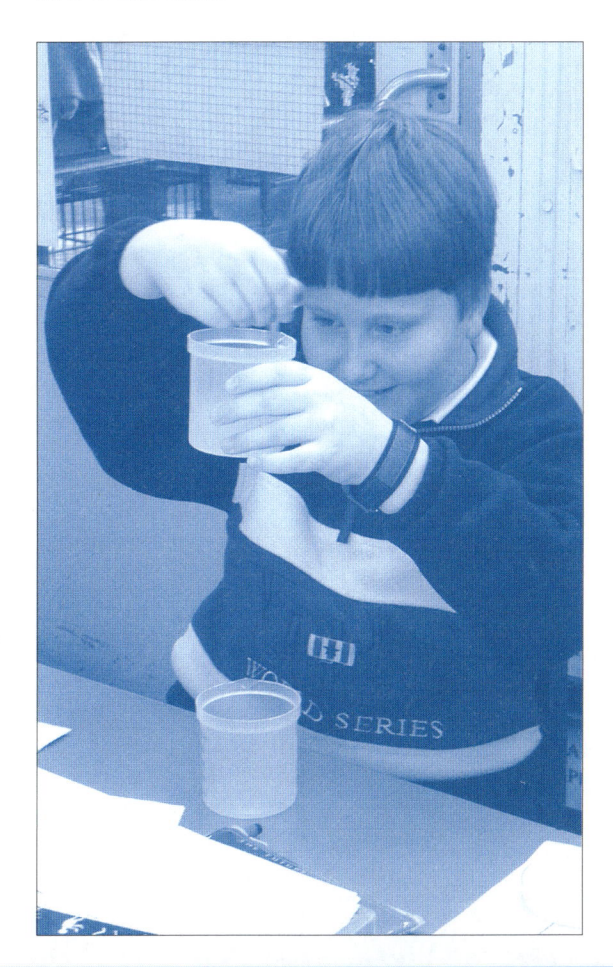

> You want to introduce the work of Van Gogh to a class of Year 2 children. You hold up a copy of his painting 'Sunflowers' and ask your question.
>
> 'Who painted this picture of sunflowers?' There is only one right answer. Each child will either know or not know the answer. Some will know, but won't be bothered to answer. Others will make wild guesses.
>
> But try a higher-order question and see where that takes you and the class.
>
> 'Why did Van Gogh choose sunflowers for this painting?' There are endless answers to this question. 'That's all the flowers he had in his garden.' 'He liked them.' 'They reminded him of the sunny weather.' 'He wanted to paint a picture that would be bright and cheerful.' And so on.
>
> You can pick up on any of these responses, children can discuss them, they can create scenarios around them, imagining Van Gogh's thought processes, for they are all acceptable and to some extent could be true. All the children can contribute and all can feel valued. At the same time their thought processes are being challenged and stretched and their imaginations fired. You are evoking empathy for the artist and the beginnings of art appreciation in the children.

You must always allow time for the children to think about the question, interpret it and consider their answer before they put up their hand. Try pairing the children and asking them to think about the question together and formulate a shared answer. Or ask each child to tell a partner the answer, and that child can voice the partner's reply, if chosen. Remind the children that there may not be a 'right' answer and that all ideas are welcome and can be discussed.

You can then encourage these questioning skills in children because when they begin to develop the ability to form such questions, the level of their thinking is also improving. It encourages advanced problem-solving skills.

This process supports self-assessment because

- children learn to challenge and take learning forward
- learning is related to 'real life' situations, giving it relevance, and clarifying the thinking process

- the teacher can assess each child's input into the work and each child can assess their own and others' work, which shows those children who are developing knowledge and skills often not otherwise obvious.

Reflection

When children know the learning objectives and the assessment criteria for their work, they can identify what they have achieved, see where they need to improve and find ways of doing it. This can be most effective when there is an opportunity to reflect on their work, related to the learning objectives. However, this time needs to be planned, integrated and given due importance.

Children benefit because

- they have a better understanding of the learning intentions
- they become more motivated and have a clearer understanding of a successful outcome
- they develop teamwork and raised self-esteem
- they accept more readily that work can be refined and improved
- they focus on their learning for longer periods of time.

You need to

- believe that the time spent allowing children to reflect and to improve their work is as valuable as time spent learning facts
- be committed to the closure of the learning gap so that children take more responsibility for their own learning.

Working with peers

Here children chose a partner to discuss their work or invite other children to comment on their work. Obviously, this is a method that needs to be introduced and modelled by the teacher so that children understand their role in this kind of assessment.

Children benefit because

- working with a trusted peer is less inhibiting
- they can talk analytically with each other
- it overcomes the fear of failure because children are no longer frightened of making mistakes
- children learn from the responses of their peers
- children develop the skills of cooperation and being a 'critical friend'.

You benefit because

- children are more open about their difficulties
- children take greater control of their learning, which leads to greater independence, less reliance on the teacher and increased motivation.

Checklists

These can be a help to those children who are just starting out on the process of self-assessment, or those with special educational needs. Set up a number of checklists that cover different groups of children and different curriculum areas or types of tasks. Laminate them and make them available as needed by the children in your class. On a whiteboard, list the points you will be marking.

In conclusion

Self-assessment skills are vital, especially in the modern world. By allowing our children to develop them we are not just equipping them to succeed at school, we are equipping them for life. By allowing children to take a stake in their learning we are empowering them, enabling them to succeed, raise their self-esteem and develop their skills in thinking, problem-solving, questioning, relationships with others and concentration and motivation.

> 'Observation and feedback is like holding up a mirror to enable colleagues to see themselves in action'. (Hughes, 1998)

So remember...

1. Self-assessment involves children being active because they need to gather information on how well they are doing and what they need to do to improve. Clarity is needed, gained from teacher feedback and what they have found out for themselves. Becoming life-long learners means that children need to be skilled at applying what they know about their current learning to future events.

2. Self-assessment is concerned with what we learn because learning takes place at any time within a lesson. Children obviously benefit from clear learning objectives and from the ability to ask the right questions.

3. Self-assessment is not only concerned with what has been learned, but also with how learning has taken place.

4. There are clear benefits in the learning process for children who are able to self-assess. They develop higher motivation and self-esteem. They see difficulties as a true sign of learning and realise that others have the same difficulties. They develop an enthusiasm for reflection as well as the skills to reflect effectively and their learning improves because they can concentrate on *how* they learn, not *what* they learn.

5. There are many different self-assessment techniques which all have a place in developing the self-assessment skills that children need.

10 Involving parents in the assessment process

There is much educational research to suggest that the more parents know about what their children are expected to learn and achieve, the more likely the children are to succeed. Information such as this has been difficult for parents to obtain, not because of any obstruction on the part of the school but because there was no common language or agreed structure within which to explain or report on children's progress.

Many parents in the past found the school curriculum remote and inaccessible. Schools were places where parents waited at the playground gate to collect their children – places where parents wouldn't dream of asking the teachers to explain why they were teaching a specific topic. Many were of the opinion that the school would eventually contact them if their child was having a problem. Many were also rather apprehensive about approaching schools and teachers due to incidents based on their own experiences as a child.

In this chapter there is information on

- why it is important to involve parents
- the statutory requirements for reporting to parents.

This chapter contains practical strategies for

- how to involve parents as a whole
- how to involve individual parents.

Why it is important to involve parents

We often talk about education being a partnership of teachers and parents for the benefit of the children. As we know, research shows us that the more involved the parents are, the likelihood is that the children will perform better. For a partnership to be successful there has to be understanding on both sides, each side being open and honest in their dealings with the other. This means that effective channels of communication need to be established and a clarity reached over how, when and for what reason information will be presented to parents, both about their own children and the school as a whole. It is worth remembering that, as well as a child's natural parents, the term 'parent' may also apply to anyone with parental responsibility for a child or anyone who has care of a child, that is, the person with whom the child lives. All parents must be treated equally and, unless there is a court order limiting an individual's exercise of parental responsibility, relevant information should be made available to all the child's 'parents', including those who do not live with the child.

Parents have a right to be informed about aspects of their child's education but, by fully involving them, the school can benefit in other ways. Well-informed parents are in a better position to work with and support the school in providing a high standard of education. Part of the school's role is devising effective ways of communicating with parents so that they are kept fully informed, and so that they can take an active and constructive part in their child's learning.

Parents also have a part to play in disclosing information to the school. As teachers we need to know why George is suddenly withdrawn and quiet, or why Nisha is refusing to take part in games lessons. Parents often know the reasons for these situations, and sharing it with the school can help us all to resolve or to respond more sensitively to a situation.

Parents can also feed back information about their child's learning. They see them tackling their homework, they know how much support they need or whether they complete it very quickly and without any real challenge. They know what they have been learning at sports clubs or scouts, and so on, and they know what books they choose from the public library.

When we can meet with the parents and share our knowledge, we end up with a broader picture of the children, their strengths and their needs.

The statutory requirements for reporting to parents

Parents have a number of rights to particular information about the school and their child's education. These should be regarded as a minimum entitlement and shouldn't be the only things you would want to share with them.

Parents have the right to receive information about schools in their area to help them express a preference in deciding the school for their children. Should the situation arise, they would also need access to information if they decide to appeal against decisions on admissions and exclusions. The school's prospectus is the main document to provide information about the school.

Another statutory document is the governing body's Annual Report to Parents. This is a good opportunity to make sure that parents receive a complete picture of the school.

Parents have the right to information about decisions concerning their child's education such as those regarding special educational needs provision. Parents also have the right to reports on their child's performance at school. At the very least they should receive an annual written report, which should include information about

- the child's progress in all curriculum subjects
- their general progress
- a record of their attendance
- the arrangements the school has made for discussing the report with teachers
- the child's attainment in any statutory National Curriculum assessments
- school and national comparative results in National Curriculum assessments.

Parents also have the right to see their child's educational record and to give notice if they wish to change or add to it if they consider the record is not accurate. Any request for such a change to a child's record should be attached to that record and become a part of it.

How to involve parents as a whole

The way that schools communicate information to parents is of vital importance. If the school seriously believes in parents as partners, then it will want to be sure that it finds the best ways of disseminating that information. This will depend on the context of the school and its families.

> One school looked at this issue and considered the following.
>
> - How can we reach as many parents as possible?
> - How readable is the information we are making available?
> - Are the design and layout user-friendly?
> - Is it available on the Internet?
> - Is it available in other languages, if required?
> - Does it make parents feel comfortable about coming into school?
>
> We decided this area was so important that we needed a specific policy with regard to our approach to parent partnership.
>
> Allied to the parent partnership policy is the home–school agreement. This explains the school's aims and values concerning the education of children and how we expect them to behave. It is also used to explain the school's responsibilities and those of parents and children. The school's governing body has consulted with parents before adopting our home–school agreement and parents are asked to sign a declaration to show that they accept their role in it. Children are asked to sign it, and it is also signed by the head and chair of governors.
>
> In the agreement we tell parents about
>
> - what they can expect from the school
> - what the school expects from parents and children
> - how they can help the school help their child
> - how they can become more involved in what happens at the school.
>
> There is information about the standards the school will provide and a reference to the school ethos and the ways in which it applies to all partners.

> One school encountered attendance problems when they tried to organise curriculum and other meetings. They decided to limit them to one a term because they discovered that these meetings were quite intimidating for some parents. Others were happy with the education the school was providing and it seemed that they only ever saw the same parents. They looked into other ways of making these meetings more attractive to all parents. First they surveyed the parents and now have several new ideas to try. One way, it seems, is to involve the children, as parents wish to support them if they are participating.
>
> They looked at the way in which they hold open meetings where parents may
>
> - learn about a particular curriculum area
> - find out more about what their child may be learning and doing in the coming term
> - learn how they can support children in the classroom
> - be given advice on how they can help their children at home
> - socialise with other parents and teachers
> - be given information about school visits
> - meet teachers from the next stage of education, before their children move on.
>
> Following the review of this type of meeting, the following guidelines were devised.
>
> - Make sure that parents know the purpose and content of the meeting.
> - Ensure that the information and activities are specific to the target audience.
> - Use a range of presentation techniques which include activities so that parents don't just sit and listen.
>
> As a follow-up to some of these meetings, the school produces information booklets – this is particularly useful for parents who can't attend for one reason or another.

How to involve individual parents

You will probably be involved in

- a meeting to discuss the Foundation Stage Profile (annually)
- a meeting to discuss a child's annual report (annually)
- an annual review for children with a statement of special educational needs (annually)
- parent consultation opportunities (termly)
- discussion of progress made for children with an individual education plan (half-termly).

It is also necessary to have an open door policy where parents can discuss issues with you as and when they arise. This should take place on the same day, wherever possible.

Parent consultation evenings

These provide the formal meetings when you spend an agreed amount of time with each set of parents and discuss the child's progress, share any concerns, set targets and agree any ways in which you can support the child at home and in school.

Make sure that you allow enough time for parents to make their contribution. If you meet with them each term you will have only that term's developments to look at. Keep focused so that you use your share of the time efficiently. Show the parents the results of any tests you have carried out and how their child is progressing towards their targets. When you set the targets at the beginning of the year, it is a good idea to build in stepping-stones so that the parents see that the child is en route to achieving them. Ask the parents if the child demonstrates any of the targeted skills at home or at outside clubs and societies he may belong to. Note these down in your records so that the parents see that you are taking their information seriously.

As part of the work involved in completing the Foundation Stage Profile, parents are asked about what their child does at home and the teacher writes this into the profile in front of the parents. They sign it as a true record. This is a policy that you may be able to adopt with these parents as their children continue through the school. The overall assessment of the child's achievements is then a combination of the knowledge that different people have about the child, and the different facets of their character and abilities that they display in different environments.

Interim meetings

Face-to-face contact with parents is important when we want to discuss particular concerns about individual children and their progress. We may also want to take the opportunity to comment on behaviour and other aspects of the child's education. There are certain principles that will make this type of meeting valuable. You should make sure, and expect, that

- parents and the school know the purpose of the meeting
- points for action have been agreed before the meeting ends

- a follow-up letter is sent, describing what was discussed, what was agreed and what will happen as a result
- parents and staff know how to contact each other, if necessary.

You should also be aware of any parents who may need special help to gain fully from this type of meeting, eg. an interpreter or help with getting to the school.

Homework

One of the biggest sources of concern among parents is the issue of homework. Parents need to know about homework and information should be contained within the school's prospectus and home–school agreement. At the start of the school year you could gather the parents together for a meeting, or send them information about how you will be setting and marking homework and the part they should be playing in it. You should

- discuss with parents your aims and aspirations regarding homework
- detail how long homework should take children and the amounts you expect them to do
- let them know the arrangements for setting homework, how it should be handed in and the way in which it will be assessed
- spend time explaining how you believe homework can contribute to a child's learning
- give ideas about what they as parents can do to support their child (parents generally want to know more about things like 'How can I help my child with reading?' or 'How do I help my child develop research skills?').

If the homework is sent home in a homework book you can include details about what is to be done, but also what you expect the children to learn from doing it. Be precise in what you expect and offer the parents the next step in case their child completes the task easily. You want to encourage parents to assess what their child has done and move their child forward in appropriate steps.

Spelling is straightforward – they must be able to spell the words by writing them down in response to a verbal instruction. The adult says the word, then repeats the word in a sentence. The child writes the word. (Give the sentence and underline the chosen word if you think your parents would appreciate this kind of help.) Parents can then test their children in the same way at home as you will be doing in school.

A mathematical problem can be more of a challenge. Here is an example. 'Take six scraps of paper and write one number from 1 to 10 / 14 to 27, etc. on each one. Stick each scrap inside one space in a half-dozen egg box. Add two tiny stones, close the lid, hold it firmly and shake it up. Open the top and see where the stones have landed. Write these two numbers down and add them up/multiply them together, and so on.' Parents need to be able to guide their own child so that they have a challenge. They mustn't, of course, make it far too difficult. You will need to set down the criteria for this. 'Start with these numbers and move on to these. Add them first and if the child gets them all right try multiplying smaller numbers.'

End of year reports

The basic contents of reports is set down by the DfES, but there is nothing to stop a school from adding more to them. It is worth considering how you can get the parents to play a more active part in this annual report of a child's achievements.

- Include a section for parents to complete with their child giving information about clubs and other outside interests.
- Include a section in which the parents can add their personal comments on the child's achievements over the year.
- Devote one of your parent consultation evenings to going through this report together. You could explain things in more detail, answer questions the parents might raise and discuss their comments with them. Together you could plan the child's next targets, based on the amount and rate of progress made over this year. At the end of the meeting you could both sign the document as an agreed record of the child's achievements.

So remember…

1. Children are more likely to achieve when the school works in partnership with parents.
2. Although there are certain statutory obligations on schools to provide information, schools who value parents as partners provide much more.
3. Schools should constantly review their practice with regard to parent partnerships in order to ensure that it remains effective.
4. Keep your parents informed about the good things their child does, as well as any concerns you may have.
5. Respect the parents' observations and knowledge of their own child.
6. Listen to what the parent has to say about how they see their child's achievements and explain about your view. Put all the information together to give a rounded picture of the child.

Appendices

Appendix one

Parent Partnership Policy Document

1 Introduction

This policy sets out what is expected of children at .... School and their parents and what they may expect of the staff. It aims to clarify the basis for these relationships in order to encourage understanding and support for each other and the school ethos. Our aim is to work successfully in partnership together and within the school ethos to provide the best possible experience for each and every child.

2 Aims

In promoting a positive partnership between home and school, we aim to

- support the ethos and values of our school
- create understanding and openness in home–school relationships
- encourage a shared commitment to the success of each child
- help parents to have a positive role in the education of their child(ren) by complementing the work of the school.

3 The school will

- ensure children are well-taught, well cared-for and treated fairly
- ensure the curriculum for Key Stage 1 and Key Stage 2 is delivered to all children
- have high expectations of children in terms of their learning, commitment and behaviour
- involve parents in solving any difficulties or problems with a child's work, relationships or behaviour at an early stage
- ensure prompt action is taken in cases of a child's misconduct or unauthorised absence
- offer parents regular information on their child's progress, through termly parent interviews
- allow parents regular access to teachers at a mutually agreeable time, particularly if a problem or difficulty arises
- provide each child with an annual report, covering all aspects of their work and progress, with spaces for comments by parents and children
- provide clear information about the school's organisation and activities
- give parents and other members of the community opportunities to learn about the curriculum and teaching methods through booklets and curriculum evenings
- give clear information about procedures for dealing with complaints
- ensure any differences in opinion are resolved through discussion and negotiation
- ensure all school policies are clearly expressed and visible in documents available from the school office.

4 We will expect that parents will

- help to sustain a child's effort and achievement
- support the school in its aims to work with and maintain the rules and ethos of the school
- make early contact with the school on any matters which might affect a child's learning, progress, welfare or behaviour, including any medical conditions such as asthma or allergies, and inform the school promptly of a child's absence
- ensure children attend regularly, are punctual and have with them any equipment they may need clearly marked with their name
- endeavour to attend parent interviews
- help to complement at home, the in-school programme of work by encouraging positive attitudes towards the school
- encourage children to complete their homework with care and to hand it in promptly
- encourage children to take advantage of any extra-curricular activities as appropriate
- ensure that children go to bed at sensible times during the school week
- keep the school informed about where they may be contacted in an emergency

- where a matter concerns them, bring this promptly to the school's attention.

5 We would expect that children will

- attend regularly and punctually
- behave in accordance with the school's ethos
- keep to the school's rules
- work hard at all times and show pride in their work by doing their best
- respect people and other people's property
- take good care of their possessions
- respect the school environment and keep the school clear from litter
- show courtesy to others
- go to bed at sensible times during the school week
- tell a parent, guardian or teacher if anything is worrying them.

6 Home–School Agreement

All parents in the school, along with their children, will be given the opportunity to participate in the Home–School Agreement which is formed by sections 2–5 above.

7 Review

This policy is subject to review on a three-year cycle by the headteacher, staff and the governing body's Staff and Pupil Care Committee.

Next Review Date: ....

Our school ethos

The ethos of a school is evident as soon as a visitor walks through the door. We believe that it is so important that it should be made specific to all that have an association with the school. We, at .... School, believe the ethos of the school and the influences it brings enables children to achieve academically and behave in a socially acceptable way.

The ethos of school influences all that come into contact with it, the children, the staff and also the parents, and this allows forms of behaviour to be worked out. We feel that by working in partnership and being open with each other, we can establish a rapport and an atmosphere of mutual support, which allows the children, their families and others involved in the school to feel secure.

Key ethos principles

- I am unique and therefore special.
- I need to be positive about myself.
- I am responsible for my own behaviour.
- It is important to learn what is right before I do what I want to do.
- I need a vision for myself and need to keep my promises to others.
- I need to listen to others.
- I need to cooperate with others.
- I should have respect for others, their feelings and opinions.
- I need to take care of myself.
- I need to be responsible for my possessions and take care of them.

The ethos is specifically taught to the children in assemblies, in class and at other times, as well as being the basis on which the school community exists.

References

Abbott, J (1999) Battery hens or free-range chickens. What kind of education for what kind of world? *Journal of the 21st Century Learning Initiative* January, 1–12.

Association of Assessment Inspectors and Advisors (AAIA) *Self-Assessment*, available from www.aaia.org.uk/publications.

Bennett, N and Kell, J (1989) *A Good Start? Four year olds in infant schools*. Oxford: Blackwell.

Black, P and Wiliam, D (1998) *Inside the Black Box: Raising standards through classroom assessment*. London: Kings College School of Education.

Carrol, L (1965) *Alice in Wonderland. The annotated Alice*. London: Penguin Books.

Cousins, L and Jennings, J (2003) *The Positive Behaviour Handbook*. London: pfp publishing.

DfEE (1998) *Supporting the Target-Setting Process*. London: DfEE.

DfEE (1999) *National Curriculum Handbook for Key Stages 1 and 2*. London: DfEE.

DfES (2001) *SEN Code of Practice*. London: DfES.

Gardner, H (1984) *Frames of Mind: The Theory of Multiple Intelligences*. London: Fontana.

Gillett, A N and Sadler, J E (1962) *Training for Teaching*. London: George Allen and Unwin Ltd.

Gregoric, A F (1982) *An Adults Guide to Style*. Columbia, CT: Gregoric Associates Inc.

Hall, N (Ed) (1989) *Writing with Reason*. London: Hodder Arnold.

Harlen, W (1993) *Teaching and Learning in Primary Schools*. London: Routledge.

Hughes, M (1998) *Closing the Learning Gap*. London: Network Educational Press.

Kolb, D A (1984) *Experiential Learning: Experience as the Source of Learning and Development*. Englewood Cliffs, NJ: Prentice Hall.

McCarthy, B (1980, 1987) *The 4MAT System – Teaching to Learning Styles with Right/left Mode Techniques*. Barrington, IL: EXCEL.

Moyle, D (1972) *The Teaching of Reading*. London: Ward Lock.

Myers, I B (1980) *Gifts Differing*. Consulting Psychologists Press.

NAHT (2000) Primary leadership. Paper No 1 (2000) *School self-evaluation*. Hobsons.

Ofsted (2003) *Good Assessment Practice in Design and Technology*. London: Ofsted.

Ofsted (2003) *Handbook for Inspecting Nursery and Primary Schools*. London: Ofsted.

QCA (2001) *Planning, Teaching and Assessing the Curriculum for Pupils with Learning Difficulties*. London: QCA.

QCA/DfEE (2001) *Supporting the Target-Setting Process*. London: QCA.

Rief, S F (1993) *How to Reach and Teach ADD/ADHD Children: Practical Techniques, Strategies and Interventions for Helping Children with Attention Problems and Hyperactivity*. London: The Centre for Applied Research in Education.

Scottish Consultative Council on the Curriculum (1996) *Teaching for Effective Learning*. Edinburgh: SCCC.

Skelton, M and Playfoot, D (1995) *The Primary File Guide to Producing School Policies*. London: pfp publishing.

Smith, A (2002) *The Brain's Behind It*. Stafford: Network Educational Press.

Smith, A and Call, N (2001) *ALPS Resource Book*. Stafford: Network Educational Press Ltd.

Stobart, G and Gipps, C (1997) *Assessment: A teacher's guide to the issues*. London: Hodder and Stoughton.

Sutton, R (1995) *Assessment for Learning*. Salford: RS Publications.

Task Group on Assessment and Testing (TGAT) (1988) *A report*. London: DES.

Tests referred to

British Picture Vocabulary Scale BPVS (nferNelson)

Primary Reading Test (nferNelson)

Edinburgh Reading Tests (Hodder and Stoughton)

Mathematics 6–14 (nferNelson)

GOAL Formative Assessment (Hodder Headline)

Lucid Research Ltd, CoPS (Cognitive Profiling System), second edition, East Yorkshire, 2001

Lucid Research Ltd, LASS Junior, East Yorkshire, 2001

nferNelson, CAT 3 (Cognitive Abilities Test 3), Windsor, 2001

To find out more about 'Accessing the P Scales' contact

Customer Support
Somerset County Council
County Hall
Taunton
Somerset TA1 4DY
Tel: 01823 355455

Additional reading

De Bono, E (1992) *Teach Your Child How to Think*. London: Penguin Books.

Fisher, R (1990) *Teaching Children to Think*. Cheltenham: Stanley Thornes.

Useful websites

www.dfes.gov.uk

www.ofsted.gov.uk

www.ncaction.org.uk

www.qca.org.uk

www.teachingthinking.net

www.aaia.org.uk